# McDonnell F-101
# Voodoo

# McDonnell F-101
# Voodoo

CANADA

## Robert F Dorr

Published in 1987 by Osprey Publishing Limited
27A Floral Street, London WC2E 9DP
Member company of the George Philip Group
© Robert F Dorr 1987

Sole distributors for the USA

*Motorbooks International*
Publishers & Wholesalers Inc
Osceola, Wisconsin 54020, USA

British Library Cataloguing in Publication Data

Dorr, Robert F.
  McDonnell F-101 Voodoo.—(Osprey air
  combat)
  1. Voodoo (Jet fighter plane)—History
  I. Title
  623.74'64    UG1242.F5

ISBN 0-85045-752-1

Editor Dennis Baldry

Designed by Gwyn Lewis

Filmset in Great Britain by Tameside Filmsetting
Limited, Ashton-under-Lyne, Lancashire and printed
by BAS Printers Limited, Over Wallop, Hampshire

**FRONT COVER**
*F-101B Voodoo, serial 58-336, of the Air Defense
Command's 29th Fighter-Interceptor Squadron over
Montana in the early 1960s*
(Maj Roger K Roberson)

**TITLE PAGES**
*CF-101B Voodoo, serial 101059/ex-USAF 57-432, of No
416 'Lynx Squadron', Canadian Armed Forces, parked at
Toronto in front of Vought A-7D Corsairs from the 107th
Tactical Fighter Squadron, 127th Tactical Fighter Wing
of the Michigan Air National Guard in September 1983.
Just after Christmas 1982, crewed by American exchange
pilot Captain Bob Slack and navigator Captain Mark
Forseille, this airplane suffered a right main gear collapse
landing at CAFB Comox (page 163)*
(Douglas R Tachauer)

# Contents

*Dedicated to*
*Captain Charles C Winston III*

# Introduction

The electrical stench and the hum of the air conditioner in Colonel Ed Taylor's trailer gave backdrop to the crack of ice cubes as Taylor refilled glasses, looked hard at Lt Col John Bull Stirling, and asked again why it had taken Stirling so long to get out here. It was June 1966 in Saigon, Taylor and Stirling elders in the fraternity of those who fly and fight, bonded now by the terrible charge of leading younger men into battle. Again, diplomacy had failed. Again, only force of arms could carry the day.

Taylor commanded the 460th Tactical Reconnaissance Wing at Tan Son Nhut airbase, bearing on his shoulders the sustained reconnaissance effort against a bitterly entrenched North Vietnam. He'd looked for Stirling, asked for him, to lead men who would fly up there in the RF-101C Voodoo. Your turn in the Barrel, they called it—flying the RF-101C to Hanoi where the only way to get the pictures was to test yourself and your Voodoo against a nation brimming with MiGs, missiles and Triple-A. The men in Taylor's wing and Stirling's squadron would confront the most intense air battle environment ever seen while carrying out the fastest combat missions ever flown. Taylor handed over the glass and said something about John Bull dragging his feet coming out to Southeast Asia from South Carolina. He said that men were dying here, and that John Bull was needed. No words existed for the ties between these men—officers, wingmen, friends; they'd shared it all—but Taylor was in a mood to goad. 'What took you so long?' he implored again. Stirling, who was forty-six years old and well-acquainted with war, replied that it was time to get on with the job and that he thought they could win.

In this volume, there appears a photo of John Bull Stirling crossing the main runway of the MiG base at Kep with everybody beneath his Voodoo trying to kill him. They didn't. The North Vietnamese inflicted painful and terrible casualties to the elite cadre who flew McDonnell's long-nosed 'One Oh Wonder', but they didn't inflict enough. In the end, every time mettle was tested on the field of battle, the North Vietnamese came up lacking. If it had been up to warriors like Stirling, rather than diplomats like me, we would have left in those smoke-filled skies a message so unmistakable that no future enemy could have read it wrongly. We would have prevented anybody from messing with the United States again and assured a *pax Americana* for the remainder of the century. Phantoms, Thuds and Stratofortresses helped to leave that message but not everyone realizes that a cantankerous and unsung airplane from a once-unknown St Louis manufacturer, flown by some of the most experienced pilots who ever sat in a cockpit, also delivered a message to Ho Chi Minh. The Voodoo was the fastest thing that ever went North and the North Vietnamese never really found a way to stop it from getting there, snapping up the pictures, and returning safely to base. The Voodoo dated literally to World War 2, as did some of its older pilots, and it was in Vietnam *first*, as early as 1961, and it could have won. No other accolade is as significant.

The F-101 Voodoo in its many variants also typified the 'century series' of supersonic warplanes which dominated the world of fighter aviation in the 1950s. In an age of atomic confrontation, there was an entire wing of Voodoos which could perform no other useful function but to drop atomic bombs. Still other Voodoos guarded against the bombers that might assault the North American continent, first in US Air Force colours and later in Canadian livery. From the beginning of its service until the end, the Voodoo was one of the fastest and most powerful aircraft in the world—yet its history goes back to the XP-88 project which was spawned only days after the end of World War 2.

When the XP-88 (later XF-88) was coming along,

David S Lewis was chief of aerodynamics for the McDonnell Aircraft Company (and later Vice President, Project Management). When the F-101 was taking shape, Sanford N (Sandy) McDonnell was a design engineer and later a design group leader on the Voodoo. In later years, Lewis became head of General Dynamics while McDonnell headed up the McDonnell Douglas Corporation. As design veteran E F Peters puts it, 'I wonder if any other airplane led to the chairmanship of the two biggest American aerospace companies.'

This volume is an attempt to capture the quintessential Voodoo. In previous histories, I have made it clear that I would attempt to discuss the weak points of an aircraft design as well as the strong. Here, the message is the opposite. The F-101 Voodoo may well have been more difficult to fly than any other fighter ever to enter widespread service. Certainly, its flaws received widespread attention. The reader is advised that I come to praise the Voodoo, not to bury it, and that the pitch-up problem, the reluctant nosewheel, and other difficulties are mentioned not for the purpose of criticizing, but in order to set forth an accurate history about an airplane that made a special mark. Because this is an 'Air Combat' series, this Voodoo chronicle is partly about airplanes, partly about men. Great men they were, the special breed who flew this magnificent airplane, and some of them happily contributed to the account which follows.

Again, a certain 'gee whiz' accompanies the flow of words across the pages which follow, the inevitable awe felt by this aviation historian toward the men who fly and fight. A glossary is appended. Military ranks and Air Force terms are given for the period of time covered. Using the correct term for a given period of time is no easy task, as a few examples will illustrate. The McDonnell Aircraft Company was called MAC by its employees in 1948, but McAir in 1968. The Air Force had Fighter-Bomber Wings in 1956, but Tactical Fighter Wings in 1959. Chappie James was a negro in 1961, a black in 1967. Throughout the pages which follow, no task has proven more difficult than the chore of using the precise term for a particular time.

This volume is almost certain to contain some errors. They are my responsibility alone. But a history like this cannot be set on paper without the help of many. It is a near-impossible task to find thanks for all who contributed.

This book is dedicated to Captain Charles C Winston III, an RF-101C pilot who paid the highest price—all honour to his name. I'm grateful to editor Dennis Baldry for proposing this project and helping in its gestation period, especially during labour. George Mills at McDonnell put me in touch with Edward M (Bud) Flesh, who designed the airplane, while Robert S (Beaver) Blake at McDonnell foraged through historical files that had not been scrutinized for years. My debt to Bud Flesh is a significant one indeed.

It is impossible to mention the F-101 Voodoo without mentioning Paul D Stevens. Paul has devoted a life to studying the Voodoo, its tribulations and its triumphs. Paul had no role in the completion of this volume, but his contributions to numerous historical publications helped me to start down the road he paved.

Assistance in the preparation of this work was received from the McDonnell Douglas Corporation, the US Air Force, the Department of State, and numerous military units.

I especially want to thank Robert J Archer, Maj Gen Fred J Ascani, Honey Connolly Baker, Duane E Boye, Lt Gen James R Brickel, Col Jack Broughton, Robert L Burns, Steve Camara, Col Ray W Carlson, Kenneth C Carter, Lt Col John R Evans, Mark Forseille, Peter Foster, Michael France, James W Freidhoff, Lt Col A Robert Gould, Lt Gen Gordon Graham, Major Nina Gustafson, Bill Gunston, Joseph G Handelman, Col Bob Hanson, Robert Hagar, Marty J Isham, Martin Judge, Lt Col Donald J Lang, Pat McCullum, Col Arthur A McCartan, David W Menard, Col Jack D Morris, Col Daniel J (Jack) Nelson, Brig Gen Robin Olds, Ralph G Paules, Walter B Pearson, George W Pennick, E F Peters, John P Reeder, Roger K Roberson, Frederick W Roos, Robbie Shaw, Col John Bull Stirling, Norman Stutts, Douglas R Tachauer, Norman Taylor, 'Deep Throat,' Jan Towney, Nick Williams, David Wrye and Emily Wrye.

The views expressed in this book are mine and do not necessarily reflect those of the Department of State or of the United States Air Force.

*Robert F Dorr*
London, November 1986

# Chapter 1
# The Trial of the Green Pythons
## Flying the RF-101C in Combat

To look at it, standing on the parking apron shimmering behind thermal waves on a hot day at Udorn, the airplane exuded sleekness and force.

The McDonnell RF-101C Voodoo was still perhaps the highest-performing warplane in the world two decades after being sketched out on paper, a decade after entering service. The product of a company that was unknown when it was conceived, the Voodoo was the butt of an airmen's bar-room ballad which called it a widowmaker and was more difficult to fly than any fighter ever to attain squadron service with the US Air Force. It was known for pitching up and it had a nosewheel that wouldn't retract, sometimes, but in addition to being a powerful fighter the camera package described later in this narrative made it an exceedingly effective flying photo platform. Those cameras and the Voodoo's instruments regularly went on the blink in Udorn's terrible heat, while its tyres disagreed mightily with the Thai airfield's concave runway and steel-plank revetments. After years in silver and gray, the Voodoo was painted finally in the T.O.114 green-brown camouflage of this widening war. And a warplane it *was*, propelled by afterburning 15,000-lb (6804-kg) thrust Pratt & Whitney J57-P-13 turbojets; it not only *exuded* speed and power, it *had* both.

At Udorn in 1966, Edward W O'Neil Jr was typical of experienced reconnaissance (recce) pilots who flew the RF-101C Voodoo and who knew that it was the only aircraft capable of penetrating the enemy's homeland now that the war had spread to fiercely-defended North Vietnam.

O'Neil was typical, too, of the Air Force officer who'd stayed in shade 84 blue during lean years when promotions were slow, rewards few—perhaps because pilots did more flying and less paperwork, perhaps because commanders led men rather than managing systems, or maybe because fast-jet aviation went through dramatic advances in an era when service to one's nation was seen not merely as honourable but inevitable. Ed O'Neil graduated from Stanford in 1950. War broke out and he joined the Air Force. He flew F-80s, RF-80s, the F-94, even the portly and fondly-loved F-89 Scorpion, before finding himself in the RF-101C Voodoo. War broke out again. O'Neil, 37, was a captain. Typical of those who flew Voodoos *before* the war heated up, he was junior in rank but had 2,000 fast-jet hours. A young man with old eyes.

The RF-101C Voodoo, as will be recounted further in this volume, was the first aircraft put into Southeast Asia combat by a US Air Force squadron. In 1961, the men of the 15th TRS (Cotton Pickers) and 45th TRS (Polka Dots) took Voodoos into Thailand, Laos and South Vietnam. Four years later, at which time the war was only beginning to expand and to appear in American headlines, the 15th TRS sent a few Voodoos up to Udorn-Thani, Thailand, when that backwater airfield with its narrow, dipping runway was known only as home for the CIA's airline, Air America. The recce mission to be mounted from Udorn was given an evocative name— Green Python.

On 21 November 1964, the first RF-101C Voodoo to be lost in combat (56-0230), operating from Saigon, was shot down by anti-aircraft fire over the Mu Gia Pass. The first loss of an Udorn-based Voodoo occurred on 29 April 1965 when an RF-101C (56-0190) was claimed by Hanoi's growing defences. In February 1965, the US began regular combat missions over North Vietnam. By 1966, O'Neil's 20th Tactical Reconnaissance Squadron had taken over the airbase at Udorn, the Green Python nickname, and a pet green snake which was usually curled up on the orderly room floor.

O'Neil's squadron commander, the Old Man, harkened from an era which pre-dated even the magnificent period in the fifties and sixties when

Voodoo pilots were the *creme de la creme*. The Old Man had flown in combat in the B-26 Marauder, no less. He, too, was the butt of a bar-room ballad but that simply proved that he was one of the good ones, one of those commanders who was out in front when it came time to fly and fight. Flying in the Barrel they called it, taking the Voodoo up to Hanoi. 'It's your turn in the Barrel,' was the actual phrase. Lt Col John Bull Stirling went up into that region of terrible danger day after day and O'Neil and the men of the squadron followed, and they would have followed him to hell itself. In 1986, out of contact for two decades, O'Neil remembered, 'My greatest commander was Stirling. He was what one needed and wanted if you were fighting a war.'

That's a quote from 1986. Some of the following, however, is from O'Neil's end-of-tour report, '*Flying in the Barrel, Summer 1966,*' which he wrote at the time and which was classified SECRET at that time. To distinguish O'Neil, age 37, from O'Neil, age 57, quotes from '*Barrel*' are italicized throughout this chapter.

Newcomer: 'But why did they choose that exact phrase, the one about it being your turn in the Barrel?'

O'Neil: 'Those who ask, don't know. Those who know don't ask.'

The war was full-blown by 1966. A typical recce mission in the Voodoo involved a dawn takeoff and $3\frac{1}{2}$ hours covering two to four targets while jinking to evade Hanoi's increasing number of missiles and MiGs. The Voodoo had a fairly comfortable cockpit, even cushioned armrests that folded down for pilot comfort, but the mission, nevertheless, meant plenty of sweat and tension. The Hanoi-Haiphong region bristled with SAM sites, MiG bases and Triple-A (anti-aircraft artillery). Pilots had developed, from combat experience, the technique of approaching the target at very low level, then applying 'burner and putting the Voodoo into a 'pop up' to 4,600 ft (1402 m) just before arrival. On afterburner, the Voodoo could remain 'high,' meaning within the performance envelope of the dreaded SAM missile, for three to four minutes before a SAM site could lock on. Though it never possessed more than sixteen RF-101Cs and usually less, in 1966 O'Neil's squadron had more aircraft than pilots—yet launched 16 to 19 sorties daily, seven days a week. Airmen calculated that it was mathematically impossible to complete 100 missions alive, and indeed it seemed so.

*The RF-101C was the first warplane put into Southeast Asia by a US Air Force squadron (in 1961). The better-known F-105 Thunderchief, or Thud, did not appear in the combat zone until three years later. This formation of Voodoos and Thuds probably took place in 1964, the Voodoos belonging to the 15th TRS (Cotton Pickers), which operated from Bangkok and Saigon early in the war (Evans)*

When he *had* survived, Ed O'Neil's principal thoughts were with those who hadn't. '*I do not believe the people who came back were lucky, but I cannot help thinking some of the people who did not return were unlucky.*' Referring to a period in May–August 1966 when RF-101C Voodoos flew unaccompanied over North Vietnam, O'Neil concluded, '*The atmosphere was hostile but [temporarily] relatively free of MiGs. However, during this time we lost three crews, very competent crews, each with over 60 missions, we lost them to something—if only we knew what.*' In August 1966, the 20th TRS at Udorn and its companion squadron at Tan Son Nhut (Saigon) reverted to the former practice of flying two-plane missions. A single aircraft failing to return might evoke an aura of mystery. If a flight of two resulted in a loss, one pilot would return and could tell the others in the close-knit Udorn community what had happened.

So far as the author is aware, the story of the Udorn-based Voodoos and their duel with North Vietnam—their time of trial—has never been told in book form. What follows, then, ahead of this volume's introduction to the technical side of the Voodoo, is a *tour d'horizon* of the testing of the 20th TRS and the Green Pythons.

## The Night Before

For the Voodoo pilot, his trial by fire began on the night before. As the bombing campaign against North Vietnam moved in fits and starts, except on the enemy's side where improvements in the defences of the Red River delta, including Hanoi and Haiphong, were relentless, the 'night before' each mission became more and more fearsome. Looking at the flight schedule, each Voodoo jock learned whether, on the following day, he would draw an 'easy counter' (known to another generation as a milk run) or his turn in the Barrel. Stirling wrote later that some pilots learning of their assignments shrugged their shoulders and ambled towards the bar while others went quietly into the toilet to be sick. O'Neil said:

'*I have been so scared under fire that I once forgot to turn "ON" my cameras (perhaps it was the fascination of seeing muzzle flashes for the first time). I have tossed and turned in the night and gagged in the morning when I brushed my teeth. I have seen men go to God, and men go to booze. I have seen a man for what he is, and a war for what it brings, and I now realize that restful, peaceful sleep is one of the most precious things in the world.*'

The confusion which underlay the conduct of the war inevitably rubbed off on the pilots at Udorn, especially when they were trying to sleep and couldn't. Nobody, Lyndon Johnson included, had defined exactly what the Rolling Thunder bombing campaign against Ho Chi Minh was supposed to accomplish. The US would eventually increase its force in South Vietnam to more than half a million men, and was proclaiming that the war could be won if aggression from the North could be halted—but Thuds were strafing individual trucks while for-

bidden to bomb a truck factory; Phantoms were being shot down by MiGs while prohibited from attacking MiG airbases. At times, the 20th TRS was 'fragged' (ordered) to get Voodoo photography of a target, at mortal risk to the Voodoo pilot, only to learn that the pictures were never used! When they *were* used, permission to attack even a target as insignificant as a lone mobile SAM site had to come from the Situation Room in the White House, via a labyrinthian chain of command which went through the Pentagon, Honolulu and Saigon. If an RF-101C Voodoo pilot was hurt, killed or captured to no purpose, that was the breaks.

## Single Ship Concept

What about sending a lone Voodoo up north, into harm's way, with no wingman to report what happened?

'*The single ship concept for reconnaissance in both highly defended and undefended targets is the most profitable employment of aircrews and aircraft and offers the following advantages:*

'*1. Manoeuvrability without wingman consideration.*

'*2. High speed low level terrain masking.*

'*3. Weather penetration at any time.*

'*4. Minimum radio transmissions.*

'*5. Maximum speed employment.*

'*6. Minimum enemy target development.*

'*7. Maximum use of fuel, i.e., wingman will normally use more fuel than leader.*

'*8. A chance to be alone in a decision and a plan.*'

The final item was paramount. Formation flying was for those less experienced weenies in Thuds and Phantoms. Individual style was everything. By the time the war broke around them, some Voodoo pilots had spent almost a decade putting the fine touches on very individual ways of flying missions.

According to Captain Wilmer P Reaves (of whom, more soon), the Old Man's boss, the commander of the 20th TRS's parent wing, Colonel Ed Taylor, had come up to Udorn from Saigon to tell RF-101C jocks that they would have to fly alone from now on because they had lost so many airplanes.

On 12 August 1966, when O'Neil's billet mate Major Blair C Wrye was shot down and killed (in RF-101C 56-0056), a pair of two-ship missions was under way. 'Blair was on PCS to the 20th TRS [permanent change of station, i.e., not on temporary assignment], thus required to do 100 missions straight with an R & R [rest and recuperation] break that never happened. He was a little ahead of me on missions. I was in the 30s, I believe, and his counters [missions which 'counted,' i.e. those over North Vietnam rather than Laos] were in the 50s. We both went deep on the day he was shot down. He had taken off approx 30 minutes prior to me on either Kep or Thai Nguyen, or vice-versa, as our targets. It was *hot*—temperature *and* activity. I lost all communications equipment because of the extreme heat generated in the comm equipment area that popped all circuit breakers. I'm sure it also happened to Blair, leaving him with no

**LEFT**
*Long, lean and mean. A variety of camouflage schemes had been tried on RF-101A and RF-101C Voodoos, long before other USAF aircraft were camouflaged. The scheme which became standard in the Southeast Asia conflict is shown here, although this RF-101C (56-0201) is seen at a European base. Paint appears to have been applied recently, judging from pristine condition of afterburner cans (USAF)*

**RIGHT**
*Captain Edward W O'Neil, Jr, 37-year-old RF-101C Voodoo pilot of the 20th TRS in the pilots' hooch at Udorn, Thailand, in August 1966. O'Neil stands at the bar. Behind him is tomorrow's flying schedule. The men do not learn their exact targets on the night before, but each learns whether his mission tomorrow will be a milk run or whether it will be his turn to confront North Vietnam's heaviest defences, flying in the Barrel (O'Neil)*

*RF-101C Voodoo pilots at Udorn in July 1966. Major Blair C Wrye, at left closest to camera, was killed in combat two weeks later. Major William D (Dave) Burroughs (centre) was shot down and captured on mission No 99. Pilot at right is unidentified. Voodoo pilot Ed O'Neil spent his career in an aircraft designed for photography, but never again clicked a shutter in his spare time. 'I stopped taking pictures after this.'*
(O'Neil)

**LEFT**
*The scene at Udorn, where the Green Pythons go to war. RF-101C Voodoos of the 20th Tactical Reconnaissance Squadron. The Voodoo was one of the first aircraft to wear camouflage and one of the last to acquire tailcodes, so this photo could have been taken in 1966 or 1967*
(Carlson)

LEFT
*Into the crucible. Lt Col John Bull Stirling, commander of the 20th Tactical Reconnaissance Squadron's Green Pythons, crosses the North Vietnamese MiG base at Kep on 19 January 1967, the second time a pair of RF-101C Voodoos went into the Barrel escorted by F-4C Phantoms using ALQ-71 noise-jamming pods. Captain Sanford L (Sandy) Sisco, the second RF-101C pilot in SAVANNAH flight, took this photo. In the escorting RATTLER flight of Phantoms, Capt J J Jayroe on his 100th mission was shot down and became a prisoner minutes after Stirling evaded no fewer than 18 SAM missiles*
*(courtesy Lt Gen James R Brickel)*

*Captain Mike Moore's RF-101C Voodoo leads a quartet of F-4C Phantoms from the 8th Tactical Fighter Wing, the Wolfpack, on a penetration deep into North Vietnam in February 1967. Throughout the war, debate continued as to whether Voodoos should go north alone, or accompanied by help*
*(Brickel)*

ability to transmit or receive. When I returned to Udorn and taxied in, a lot of people were lining the taxiway. What a welcome, I thought at first. But no, they were checking tail numbers. When they saw mine, they knew Blair would not be returning.'

## Shootdown and Capture

During the 1965–68 Rolling Thunder operations against North Vietnam, 100 missions 'up North' was the magic figure that would give a Voodoo pilot his ticket on the Freedom Bird, the airliner that would take him home. In the interim, capture by the North Vietnamese was a prospect almost as grim as death. Twelve RF-101C jocks paid the highest price. For ten others who became prisoners of war (POWs), being shot down in 1966 meant *eight years* of captivity, of torture, of being denied medical treatment, of being paraded through angry crowds in Hanoi, used as a political pawn, stoned, starved, beaten. In common with Thud pilots operating from

Takhli and Korat, Voodoo pilots at Udorn not merely *knew*, they *believed* that it was statistically impossible to complete 100 missions over North Vietnam. They also believed, because they *had* to believe, that life itself hung on every man carrying his share of the load.

Captain Billy Boyd and O'Neil were talking about what it would be like to be shot down and interrogated. Billy was known for his gastronomic tastes. O'Neil: 'If they were putting pressure on you to sign false propaganda statements about germ warfare, how long do you think you could hold out?' Boyd: 'Oh, Ed, I could hold out. Don't worry about me.' O'Neil: 'But *how* long?' Boyd: 'Oh, about three hours past supper.' It was gallows humour. The POWs held out for the whole eight years.

O'Neil's squadron had a policy. If you'd completed 95 missions, your last five would be the 'piece of cake' variety in the easy areas of North Vietnam, known as Route Packages One and Two. Captain William D (Dave) Burroughs drew the Bac Ninh Bridge on

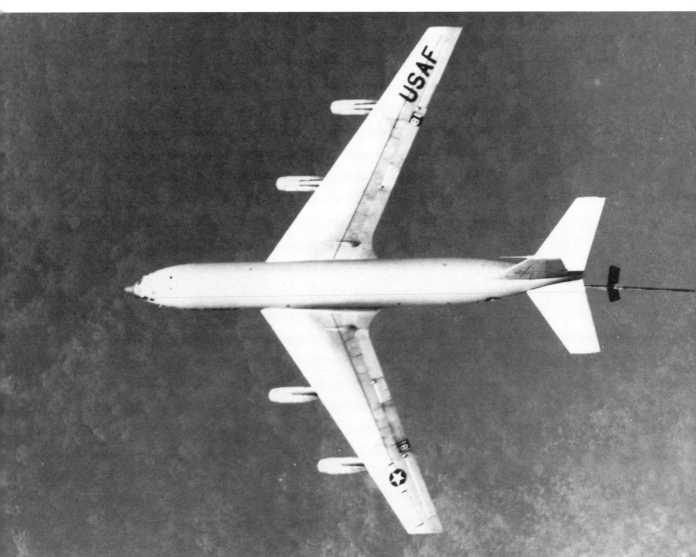

ABOVE
*Ready for a mission, RF-101C Voodoo is primed in the revetment at Udorn, from which the Green Pythons of the 20th TRS mounted their missions against North Vietnam. Long-nosed Voodoo's camera bay permitted the aircraft to carry a variety of cameras for pre- and post-strike coverage of targets. Up to three 450 US gal (1700 lit) ventral fuel tanks could be carried and Voodoo had both 'flying boom' and 'probe and drogue' in-flight refuelling systems*
(SMSGT Carroll Garrison)

LEFT
*They weren't always accessible when needed, but Voodoo pilots never failed to praise the tanker crews who got them home when the fuel was nearly depleted. An RF-101C Voodoo of the 20th TRS tries to mate with a KC-135 over Laos, returning from a combat mission 'up North.' Throughout the war, KC-135 Stratotankers remained under the jurisdiction of SAC, rather than local field commanders*
(Carlson)

mission # 99. It was a scheduling error. Burroughs wasn't supposed to go up there, not up into the Barrel. On 31 July 1966, without uttering a word about the mistake, Burroughs launched in his RF-101C Voodoo (56-0226), went north, and was hit by Triple-A. There was never the faintest hope of rescue. Burroughs was a POW until March 1973—'a real hero,' says O'Neil.

In 1966, seasoned RF-101C Voodoo pilots saw a sudden and dramatic change. Until then, the Voodoo had been flown by men who were among the most experienced in the Air Force. Says Lt Col Bob Hanson, 'They were of a calibre never to be seen again in the Air Force because they were true professionals. These people weren't bright young "Zoomies" on the way up and "getting their cards punched in the right jobs." They were professional fighter pilots and knew their jobs like no others.'

In mid-1966, the Udorn-based squadron was suddenly acquiring pilots with little experience, ill-prepared and unready for the difficult Voodoo and the dangers of North Vietnam. To quote one of the new guys, who later completed *his* 100 Voodoo missions, 'I had spent my time in ATC [Air Training Command] flying as an instructor in T-birds and Tweets [T-33s and T-37s], so I was excited about sitting in the procedures trainer in the corner of one of Kadena's hangars [Kadena AB, Okinawa] for about five hours and then walking out to my single seat Century Series RF-101C and actually *flying* that hummer!'

The new guys were good guys, but that didn't ease the gloom at Udorn. Says O'Neil, 'Jim Murphy, an old friend of mine since 1953 days, ran the RF-101C RTU [replacement training unit] at Shaw AFB [South Carolina]. He wrote to me while I was at Udorn in 1966 and asked what could RTU training do to better prepare the aircrews for SEA operations. My reply was, "Stop sending us bomber retreads with 50 hours. Tap those ADC [Air Defense Command] F-101B jocks who have Voodoo experience." This was not done to the fullest—a real blunder.'

Adds Stirling, 'Since the policy was 100 combat missions a high attrition of experienced pilots resulted. The RF-101C was [no longer] in production so training aircraft had to come from existing resources. Until new pilots could be trained, the 20th TRS was largely manned by experienced recce pilots from other units on temporary duty status [like Burroughs]. The new pilots who ultimately reported to the 20th TRS were of marginal ability.'

Many years of pride, preparation and camaraderie were shattered by this change. Worse, the assignment of inexperienced pilots to RF-101C cockpits, more than a decade after the type's entry into service, had another effect. It undermined the individualism that was the hallmark of the lone recce pilot. Until then,

no two RF-101C jocks had ever flown the same mission the same way. Now, standards might be needed. Certainly, advice was needed. So Ed O'Neil wrote a primer.

## Over the Target

'*High altitude flying in a SAM area is out of the question. Although the probability of the enemy launching against a single ship is much less than their launching against a flight, you can expect a launch of up to three SAMs (minimum separation 6 seconds) at any time you fly above tree top level.*

'*How can you effectively acquire a target in a highly defended, high-threat SAM area? Flying at 4,600 to 8,000 feet [1402 to 2438 m] jinking, jinking heavily, until you're almost sick, works.*' Low-level terrain hugging was taken for granted by Voodoo veterans a generation before other airmen were forced to learn the skill. But O'Neil was careful to explain what he meant by low. '*When you get down "in the weeds," don't get so low that flying becomes more dangerous than the enemy. I mean below the peaks in the mountains and about 50 feet [15 m] in the flatlands. You fly in the weeds except over major roads, railroads and rivers—at these points you "pop," jinking, up to at least 4,600 feet [1402 m], then descend, jinking, back to the weeds. Two minutes after getting into the defences surrounding your target, you hit ABs [afterburners], pull the trigger for the cameras, and "pop up," jinking and looking. You keep all cameras going and continue to jink up to altitude for your target.*'

O'Neil cautioned the new guys not to overfly the target if it was a bridge, since less risky oblique photography could provide the needed recce pictures. Against smaller targets like barracks and SAM sites, where only vertical photography would do, he urged minimum exposure to the enemy's defences. '*Jink as you climb, jink as you level, over-fly the target, roll wings level, hit the extra picture switch, jink, and get out.*' He warned Voodoo pilots to stay away from

ABOVE
*RF-101Cs of the 20th TRS usually operated singly or in pairs, so this kind of mass refuelling was unusual on a combat mission over Southeast Asia. Even more unusual is the fact that these Green Pythons wear the experimental camouflage developed prior to Southeast Asia experience. KC-135 Stratotanker (57-1418) provides life-giving gas as Voodoos proceed on recon missions against North Vietnam*
(Norman Taylor collection)

LEFT
*When they weren't challenging Ho Chi Minh's defences up north, Voodoo pilots fought their war over endless expanses of jungle in South Vietnam and Laos. RF-101C of the Udorn-based 20th TRS on a low-level combat mission*
(Carlson)

OVERLEAF
*The Bac Giang railroad yards, a key target of US warplanes, as seen from the camera of an RF-101C Voodoo of the 20th TRS*
(Carlson)

PAGES 24–25
*Typical reconnaissance photo by an RF-101C of the Green Pythons. Taken with KA-1 camera, this view of the North Vietnamese MiG airbase at Hoa Loc shows the airfield under construction. Parking revetments for fighters ('5 ftr rvts') are evident in the centre of the picture*
(Carlson)

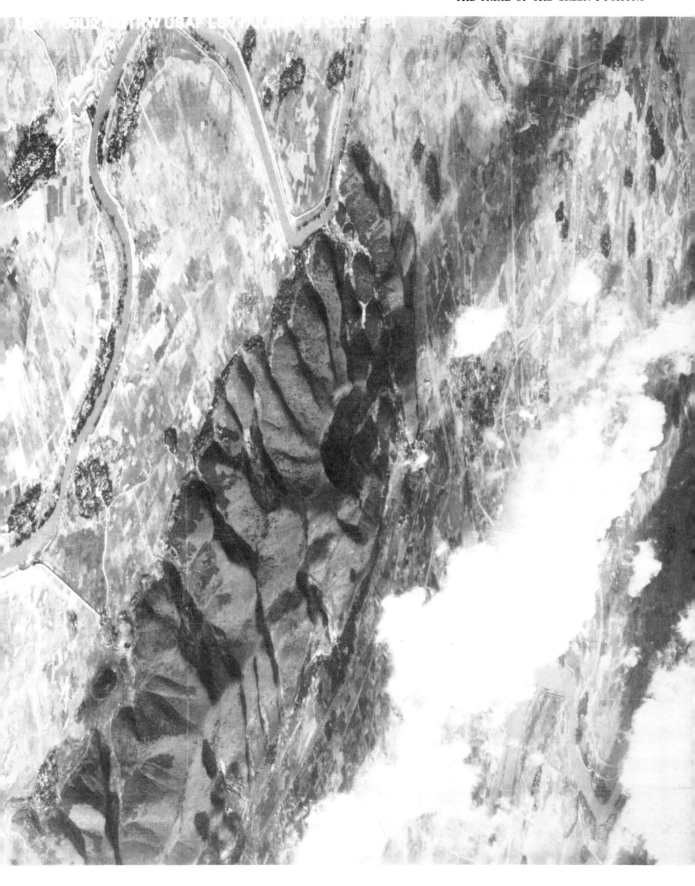

CONSTR EQUIP
PARKING AREA

PARKING
APRON

RWY UNDER
CONSTR

U/AAA

5 F

L/AAA
0616 $ H0246

PROB E/C RA

U/AAA

L/AAA
0616 $ HO

2 RECONNAISSANCE TECHNICAL SQUADRON
PHOTO: SELECT          RTE SEQ: 213A
HOA LAC AFLD AAA SITE
S: 21 01 20        N 105 30 40        E
0616 $ H0245   TOT NR: NONE
J NR: NONE          TOT: 0955        O
A: KA-1              F.L.: 36          in.
7,000          ft. SCALE: 1:5,700
        CONFIDENTIAL OP-1

20JUN67 36 CONF CF1

12,000 feet (3658 m) altitude anywhere in the target area because that was the roll-in altitude used by Thuds and the enemy had figured that out.

## Getting Hit

O'Neil advised the new guys that once they'd photographed their target, it was no time to loiter. '*Get out and get home, keeping out of the hostile area and on the deck. Don't go after bonus targets.*

'*What about hits? Hits must be expected, and strangely enough small-arms hits in the aircraft are not usually felt. You will know if a 37-mm [shell, or larger] gets a good hit, and if you are hit, no matter what type hit, Go Home! You never know the damage it has caused and going home is the only answer. Let everybody on our side [friendly aircraft in the region] know you were hit, in case you have to eject and be rescued.*'

Later in the war, combat rescue operations were carried out in North Vietnam with fair success. At this time, however, a Voodoo pilot who went down near his target might just as well not bother to use his hand-held PRC-90 survival radio. The notion of rescue was simply a pipe dream.

On 28 June 1966, Captain Wilmer P Reaves was assigned to a solo RF-101C post-strike recce mission against the longest bridge in North Vietnam, the rail

and road crossing at Viet Tri. Major James H Kasler, Korean war ace (six MiG-15s) and much-respected Thud pilot—soon, too, to become a POW—led eight F-105Ds of DODGE flight against the bridge with 750-lb (340-kg) bombs. Reaves was flying Voodoo 56-0215 and using the callsign CADILLAC.

Once DODGE flight had paid its visit and was on egress, Reaves went in. Clouds broke and the whole Hanoi valley opened up before him. He went down. He was low enough to see a lone North Vietnamese standing on a hilltop shooting at him with a rifle!

Lining up on the bridge, Reaves began to get receiverscope warnings that he was being stalked by the *Fire Can* radar associated with 85-mm anti-aircraft guns. He also had warning indications of SAM-associated *Fan Song* radar. He banked, settled into his run-in over the target, and found himself piercing a solid wall of exploding flak. Reaves' Voodoo bucked and wobbled as its port engine was badly damaged and his navigation systems went completely out.

Just past the bridge, he saw the bright red burn of a SAM sustainer engine. The SAM rushed at him and missed. He jinked and another SAM went by without exploding. Though it scarcely mattered since the flak had already crippled his plane, Reaves said later that he was engaged by the advanced Soviet missile

*SA-2 SAM missile blowing up beneath an RF-101C*
*Voodoo over North Vietnam in April 1967*
*(*Brickel*)*

**LEFT**
*RF-101C Voodoo pilots devised a manoeuvre called the*
*'pop up' to enable them to stay below the operating*
*envelope of the SAM missile except whilst directly over*
*target. This SA-2 SAM was photographed by Lt Col*
*James R Brickel on 21 May 1967, looking west towards*
*the Black River in North Vietnam*
*(*Brickel*)*

known as the SA-3. In fact, only the SA-2 type was in
service in North Vietnam then. His pictures taken
but his Voodoo gravely damaged, Reaves reversed
course and began to egress the target area, the Voodoo
following its own shadow across the river. Machine-
gun tracers followed him. Then, suddenly, the SAM
radars went off. With no compass or instruments,
Captain Reaves took the RF-101C Voodoo up to
18,000 ft (5486 m), cranked his head around to look
for MiGs, and began thinking that he'd be lucky to
get across the Mekong River into Thailand before
having to eject. If a pilot could do *that* much, a
Udorn-based HH-43F Pedro rescue chopper would
be within range.

Reaves' luck held. He made a shaky landing on

27

*RF-101C of the 20th TRS (Green Pythons) over Southeast Asia in 1967 (Carlson)*

LEFT
*Photo taken by RF-101C Voodoo pilot Lt Col James R Brickel of the 20th TRS shows an SA-2 missile detonating over Hanoi on 21 May 1967. Pilots could usually out-manoeuvre the SAM when they saw it coming. But radar warning receivers (RWR) on the Voodoo were never fully effective and it was possible to be caught by surprise (Brickel)*

Udorn's notorious runway. One of Kasler's F-105D pilots had diverted to Udorn with a hit from an 85-mm shell that had blown away most of the empennage of his Thud. Both pilots watched a PI (photo interpreter) unroll Reaves' recce film across a glass frame. With but two exceptions, Kasler had taken down every span of the bridge. Reaves' photography also showed Triple-A sites with a layer of smoke veiling the guns, meaning that they were firing, and of the Star of David-shaped SAM sites. For pressing on despite flak damage, Reaves was awarded the Silver Star.

QRC-160 noise jamming pods, employed briefly by Voodoos in combat the previous year, had been worse than useless. 'Pure junk,' one pilot called them, and they were hastily withdrawn. What Reaves called a receiverscope was, in fact, the APR-25/26 radar warning receiver (RWR), a panel-mounted scope first fitted to Udorn RF-101Cs in May 1966 and nicknamed a 'Chinese TV.' The APR-25 only provided the pilot with knowledge that a radar emission was strobing his Voodoo but was not specific enough to do more than confuse and distract him. When the APT-26 variation of the RWR became functional, the Voodoo pilot could discriminate *Fan Song* and *Fire Can* emissions. The pilot's earphones were also rigged with a distinctive aural warning for the two types of North Vietnamese weaponry radar. Later in the conflict, ALQ-51 deception jammer pods became available to Voodoo crews.

Not every man was mentally equipped to strap himself into a single cockpit, ignite twin burners, and launch against the most intense flak, the heaviest defences, in the world. Some of the men new to the Voodoo proved, however, that courage did not necessarily require experience. When Lt Col James R

29

Brickel joined the 20th TRS at Udorn in November 1966, it quickly became apparent that although he was relatively new to the aircraft type, he had both the talent and the tenacity for RF-101C missions up North. Unlike anyone mentioned so far in this narrative, yet in common with many who flew the Voodoo, Jim Brickel would finish his Air Force career with the three stars of a lieutenant general on his shoulders. In 1966, he was a graduate of the Naval Academy at Annapolis who had cut his teeth on the F-86 Sabre in several postings, spent a period in the space programme, and then transitioned to the Voodoo. Brickel camped out in the trailer next to squadron commander Stirling (who was also Saigon-based Ed Taylor's deputy *wing* commander), learned that he was close enough to hear Stirling playing the guitar he enjoyed, and helped other pilots to compose a vocal work entitled 'Ballad of John Bull, A Voodoo-Driving Man.' Still ahead for the Green Pythons lay the day when John Bull Stirling would take his Voodoo over the MiG base at Kep. Still ahead, too, lay the moment when Jim Brickel would take command of the squadron.

At a time when fighter pilots (including the recce variety) were fighting and dying, bomber pilots were running the Air Force. A SAC weenie, as Strategic Air Command people were called, met both Stirling and Brickel on an inspection trip to Udorn. Stirling had already noted that the base was growing like topsy, half of the people stationed there were busy supporting each other while only a relatively few went up to Hanoi, and Udorn's ever-increasing need for air conditioning was using up more energy than the war against North Vietnam. In World War 2, Stirling had fought the Japanese from airbases with tin Quonsets or wooden buildings and the possession of an electric fan had been a luxury. This, however, was the first air-conditioned war. And the visiting SAC weenie seemed to fit with the airbase's growing demands for administrative support, rather than with actual combat against the heavily-defended Hanoi-Haiphong region. 'So why do they use those precise words,' inquired the visiting SAC officer. 'You know, about it being your turn in the Barrel?'

Stirling did not answer. Brickel did not, either.

Ed O'Neil had known from the beginning that there was no way to explain it to someone who hadn't been there—who hadn't pitted his RF-101C Voodoo against missiles, MiGs and Triple-A. His classified 'how to' paper went on for pages, offering advice on every detail of the mission against Hanoi, but in the end he could only wish the new guys well.

*'What will your flight be like? Well, you won't have MiG cover [fighters to protect you from MiGs]. Only under ideal conditions will you get a [KC-135] tanker. And ELINT [information about the enemy provided by*

*RF-101C Voodoo of the 20th TRS with airbrakes open over Udorn in 1967*
(Carlson)

LEFT
*Members of the 20th TRS at Udorn in March 1967, near the end of the period when Lt Col John Bull Stirling was in command, marking their 5,000th combat sortie. Not long thereafter, as depicted in photo on page 179, the number of missions rose to 7,100. RF-101C Voodoo (56-0219) in background survived the war*
*(Brickel)*

BOTTOM LEFT
*The Polka Dots were in the war too. RF-101C Voodoo (56-0096) of the 29th TRS at Shaw AFB, SC, is seen at McClellan AFB, California, in September 1965 on its way to join the 45th TRS (Polka Dots), which operated from Saigon's Tan Son Nhut airport*
*(S Kraus via Norman Taylor)*

BELOW
*During the 1966–67 period, while the Green Pythons fought near Hanoi, other Voodoo pilots continued their longstanding guard in Europe. Wearing an early camouflage scheme which pre-dates the war, RF-101C (56-0228) of the 17th TRS prowls the skies of Germany in the winter of 1967*
*(Col R Tiffault via Norman Taylor)*

electronic intelligence] will seldom be around. So you're on your own, fellow, really on your own. If you're lucky, you'll not be the last man of the day in the valley. Maybe some strikes will be going on. If they are, then expect some MiGs, but lucky for you, most of the [MiG] action will be on the Thuds, so maybe you can slip in and out with little trouble. If you have to go in one or two hours after the strike, they'll be waiting for you, so remember, be prepared, you're not fooling anyone. When you "pop," the guns will be manned and they'll look like strobe lights in a circle, or as one fellow put it, "They're welding down there." You'll see it, you'll see where the flak is bursting sometimes grey and sometimes black with fireballs in the centres. They're shooting at you, fella, and all the training and skill that you have acquired is directed towards this moment. So Good Luck!!!!
'IT'S YOUR TURN IN THE BARREL!'

# Chapter 2
# The Day of the Silver Orphans
## Taking the XF-88 to Nowhere

Days after the end of World War 2, US Army Air Forces (USAAF) came to James S McDonnell's unproven company in a Missouri cow town with a contract for a new pursuit fighter, the XP-88. The USAAF wanted a 'penetration' fighter to escort the bomber force which would become Strategic Air Command (SAC) on 21 March 1946. Its contract was the first step on a path which, for years, would seem to lead nowhere. Much later, when pursuits had become fighters, the McDonnell airplane would face a 'fly off' competition with the Lockheed XF-90 and North American YF-93A, and win, hands down. Even before the other airplanes existed, the McDonnell product proved itself again and again. Nowhere was exactly where it got, in terms of a production contract, but the name Voodoo was created and in St Louis a fighter dynasty was launched, the name McDonnell to remain unproven for not much longer. To this day, Hornets, Harriers and Eagles are manufactured by the McDonnell Aircraft Company, despite an annoying stylism—used, among others, by the firm itself and by this publisher—of labelling them McDonnell Douglas products.

McDonnell and his people, although inexperienced, felt able to design and build the pursuit ship to accompany SAC's Superfortresses all the way into Soviet Russia. The chief engineer at McDonnell's airplane division, Kendall Perkins, a thin and unassuming man, was simply the best in the business. Better still, by August 1946 McDonnell had engaged the services of Edward M (Bud) Flesh, an engineer with considerable experience and a strong interest in emerging jet-engine, swept-wing technology. Flesh had begun his career with Perkins at Curtiss Aircraft in St Louis, had more recently served at that firm's Columbus plant on the unsuccessful XP-87 Blackhawk project, and was glad that Perkins—now with McDonnell—had lured him back to his home town. 'His role [Perkins] in the XP-

88 was mostly to bring me up to date on the airplane since I was so new to the company.' As project engineer on the XP-88, Flesh 'had an expert team of men assisting in the design, too numerous to mention.'

In Bud Flesh's own words, 'Until 1946, McDonnell had been strictly a Navy supplier. [In fact, before starting on the XP-88, McDonnell had not built any production airplane for anybody]. In 1946, the Air Force awarded McDonnell a contract to build a penetration fighter. [It] had to carry a great quantity of fuel to follow bombers long distances and to fight off enemy planes.' The USAAF invitation to bid in a penetration fighter competition came on 28 August 1945, not even two weeks after Japan's surrender. On 13 October 1945, a proposal, the McDonnell Model 36, was submitted to the USAAF's Air Materiel Command (AMC) for evaluation.

On 1 April 1946, under Perkins, work began on the new fighter. On 7 May 1946, a letter of intent was filed. The go-ahead came on 20 June 1946 with what is officially called 'contract W-33-038-ac-14582, quantity 2, job order 2135,' for construction of two Model 36 flight vehicles, designated XP-88 and assigned USAAF serials 46-525/526.

Perkins, Flesh and other McDonnell and Air Force people met on 21 August 1946 to complete a three-day inspection of the full-scale mockup of the XP-88. In the expectation of the day, the plane would wing merrily along beside SAC bombers flying high and deep into the Soviet Union. The notion seems fanciful now, but it did not then. It is worth noting that bomber men like General Curtis E LeMay enjoyed a dominant role in the post-war American air arm, a dominance which would continue to the day when SAC weenies were inspecting fighter bases in Southeast Asia. With the lean budgets of peacetime and the high cost of the bomber men's B-36 and B-47,

TOP

*Mystery photo. Freshly uncovered for this volume, this picture in McDonnell design shops shows an early XP-88 Voodoo concept—but which one? Company records say the photo was taken in May 1946, three months before a full-scale mockup of the XP-88 was examined. Voodoo designer Bud Flesh is almost certainly wrong in remembering this as a 'low-speed wind tunnel model of the nose section of the XP-88,' since the model appears to be made for display rather than tests*
*(MDC)*

*The beginning. On 21 August 1946, McDonnell and US Army Air Force people finish three days of inspecting a mockup of the proposed XP-88 penetration fighter. In centre is Kendall Perkins, who will later become McDonnell's vice president for engineering. At his side is Edward M (Bud) Flesh, recently lured away from the XP-87 Blackhawk programme at Curtiss Aircraft, and later to be designer of the F-101 Voodoo*
*(MDC)*

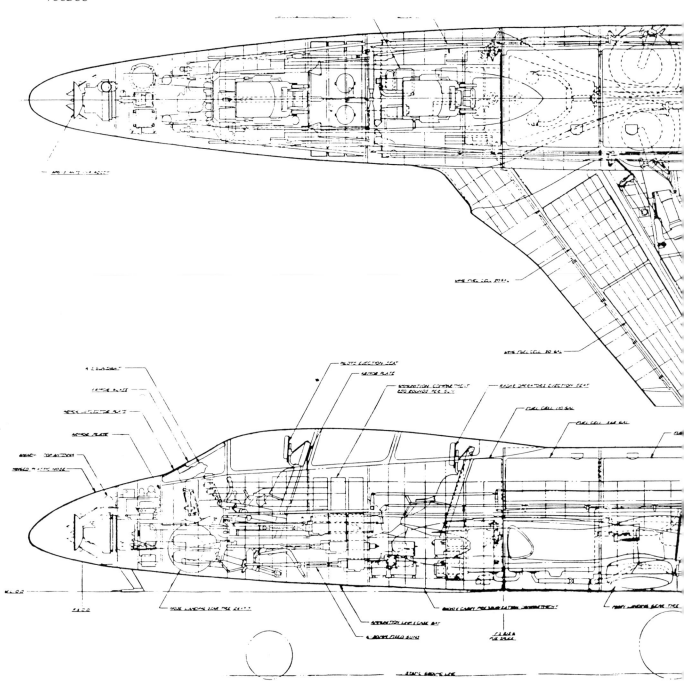

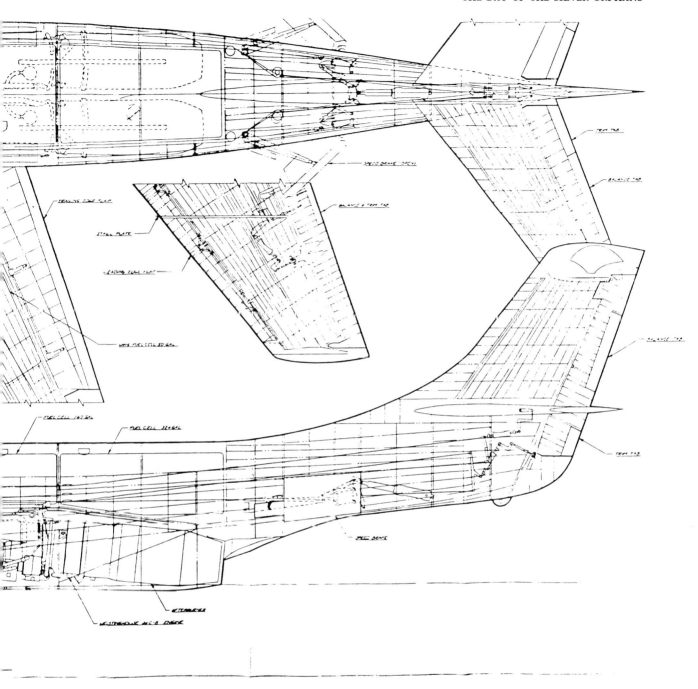

*1948 interior arrangement drawing by McDonnell's H N Cole of a proposed two-seat 'all-weather fighter' based on the XF-88 Voodoo. Not dissimilar in appearance to the F-101B Voodoo interceptor which came years later, this drawing proves that the company was thinking early about having a crew of two in the 'long bird.'*
*(MDC)*

*A 'wing flow' model of the XF-88 tested at transonic speeds by the National Advisory Committee for Aeronautics (NACA) for the Air Force in 1948. The model, on a strain gauge balance underneath a wing panel of an F-51D Mustang, was operated through an angle of attack range as the Mustang was dived to about Mach 0.8. Tests on an actual aircraft were necessary because wind tunnels at the time 'choked' in the desired Mach range (courtesy John P Reeder)*

There were rumours about closing Columbus so I contacted McDonnell and was offered the job on the XP-88. Curtiss-Wright was getting ready for the mockup on the XP-87 and they asked me to stay until that was over. Almost a month later, the same group of men came to the XP-88 mockup at McDonnell and upon seeing me one of them asked, "Do you have a twin brother up at Curtiss?"'

On 21 November 1947, a structural review was completed. It was time to cut metal. Meanwhile, on 30 June 1948, McDonnell report S-217, classified SECRET, proposed a US Navy carrier-based version of the new fighter, which had now been redesignated XF-88. To meet the demands of carrier-deck operations, the final XF-88 configuration (of which, more below) was altered. Provisions for wing tip tanks along with the controls and supporting structure for the tip tanks were removed. The fin tip antenna was shortened by 6 inches making the maximum height of the airplane less than 17 feet (5.2 m). The fuselage nose forward of the cockpit pressure bulkhead was equipped with hinges for rotating the nose section of the airplane. Wing fold mechanism and hinges, and a strengthened undercarriage for punishing carrier operations, were added. At the time, the US Navy was committed to the XF2H-1 Banshee, another product which was making the McDonnell name better known and a machine to be tested in anger in Korea. The Banshee was a practical, straight-wing fighter which looked exactly like the XF-88 would have, had Flesh not intervened with German-developed sweptwing technology. The carrier-based XF-88 was not to be.

## Design of a Voodoo

McDonnell had built planes named Phantom (FH-1), Banshee (F2H-1), and, soon, Demon (F3H-1). The name Voodoo was, perhaps, inevitable for the Air Force stable mate to these Navy fighters. In creating the XF-88 Voodoo, Perkins and Flesh tried to make a conscious choice about when to be bold, when to be conservative.

Says Flesh, 'We were bold in designing surfaces with sweep-back and minimum thickness, irreversible power controls, and [later] our own afterburner. On the other hand, we chose a conservative size, location and configuration for the tail, high lift devices, landing gear and for most of the other design characteristics.' The design had to meet a requirement of the US Air Force (which had split from the Army to become an independent service on 18 September 1947) for a penetration fighter with a combat radius of at least 900 miles (1440 km) and a fighter performance over the target good enough to cope with anticipated enemy opposition. Neither Flesh nor anyone else could yet 'anticipate' the MiG-15, which was already flying, but Flesh knew that 'these two requirements, one for long range and the other for high performance, were obviously in deep

the 'fighter men' had little influence and any fighter was more likely to succeed if its role was pegged to the strategic standoff with the Soviets. In 1946, Moscow was three years away from exploding an atomic bomb, but evidence abounded that the former ally was now the adversary in a superpower confrontation.

Bud Flesh remembers an interesting anecdote from the XP-88 mockup meeting. 'I had been with Curtiss-Wright for 17 years when they closed their St Louis plant. I was sent to Buffalo and *that* plant was closed. I was then sent to Columbus, Ohio, and made project engineer on the [Curtiss] XP-87. With all the moving around the country my wife became ill.

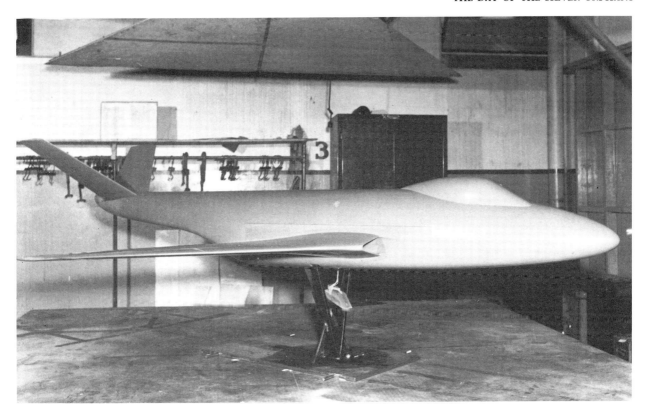

*A September 1946 model (not a mockup) of the original XP-88 Voodoo with a butterfly, or Vee-shaped tail configuration. McDonnell also proposed a US Navy, carrier-based version of the Voodoo and was also working on a proposal for a two-seat F-88 (MDC)*

conflict.' From the beginning, Flesh doubted that an upper limit of 15,000 lb (6810 kg) for combat gross weight could be observed.

The first tentative design for the XF-88 had a fuselage almost identical to the XF2H-1 Banshee with engines buried in the wing roots and with wings and tail swept a mere 20 degrees, the trailing edge being unswept. A second proposal was similar but neither was actually shown to the Air Force. The third design, which *was* presented, reflected Flesh's interest in the new technology.

'At about this time we were receiving microfilm reports of German research on the aerodynamics of swept surfaces and had translated enough to know the effectiveness of large angles of sweep and to have gained confidence in the feasibility of designing swept surfaces.' In Germany, more tests had been made at a sweep angle of 35 degrees than at any other. 'To use less didn't offer much gain [over straight wings]. To use more seemed foolhardy.' A very thin, 35-degree swept wing was decided upon.

## Engine Location

'It was with considerable reluctance that we abandoned the idea of locating engines in the wing roots as we had in [the FH-1 Phantom and F2H-1 Banshee]. This would have left more space inside the fuselage in that valuable area near the centre of gravity where it is always badly needed, particularly for fuel. It would have permitted a shorter and straighter inlet duct.' In the end, 'the engines were

placed in the bottom of the fuselage because the engine accessories were on the bottom and could be more readily reached from underneath, and because the engines could be removed from below by means of a dolly.'

A little-known fact is that the version of the XF-88 first submitted to the Air Force had a butterfly, or Vee tail. The idea was to reduce the number and improve the nature of tail intersections where compressibility effects were likely to give trouble. Early in wind tunnel tests, however, Flesh's engineers encountered adverse rolling moments due to rudder action and insufficient longitudinal stability near the stall. A more conventional tail was tested in the tunnel and when it was found to be largely free of aerodynamic faults it was chosen instead of the Vee tail. Years later, it is impossible to know whether this seemingly minor engineering decision, had it gone the other way, would have solved the pitch-up problem for which a later Voodoo was notorious.

The XF-88 was designed with speed brakes located on each side of the fuselage above and behind the engines.

The planned 350 US gallon (1300 litre) wing tip tanks for the XF-88 proved to create flutter problems. The second airframe (46-526) was exten-

sively photographed at St Louis in January 1949 fitted with these wing tip tanks (and, peculiarly, no national insignia) but it has proven impossible to locate anyone who remembers whether the airplane ever flew with the tanks. 'It was concluded that it would be impracticable from a flutter and deflection standpoint to install such large tip tanks on an airplane with swept wings thin enough to fly at high speeds.'

Rolled out at St Louis on 11 August 1948, the XF-88 does not appear unorthodox, not in retrospect. It was a low/mid-wing monoplane with 35-degree swept wings and tail surfaces, a lengthy fuselage to house fuel for the penetration role, and two 3,000-lb (1361-kg) thrust Westinghouse XJ34-WE-13 turbo-

*Only weeks after its designation was changed from XP-88, the first XF-88 (46-525) was rolled out at McDonnell's St Louis facility on 11 August 1948. The clean lines and sleek shape hid the fact that the XF-88 was sorely underpowered. This airframe later became the XF-88B turboprop testbed (MDC)*

RIGHT
*McDonnell chief test pilot Robert M Edholm, who made the first flight in the XF-88 aircraft (46-525). Not a tyre-kicking risk-taker, Edholm was cautious and courtly, and at times wore a bow tie neatly affixed beneath his flight suit (MDC)*

jets mounted in the lower centre fuselage. There was, as yet, no afterburner.

## First Flight

On 20 October 1948, the first airplane (46-525) went aloft at St Louis with McDonnell chief test pilot Robert M Edholm at the controls. With its flush exhaust area indicating the absence of afterburner, the XF-88 was a sleek and impressive sight beating up Lambert-St Louis Municipal Airport at low level. But even in the days before its famous arch or the ascendancy of its Cardinals football team, the Mississippi River cow town was not yet the right place to use the right stuff in testing the new fighter.

The scene shifts, then, to Muroc Dry Lake, twenty miles (32 km) from Rosamond in southern California, named in reverse for the Corum brothers who settled the area. During the war, Muroc had begun to supplant another airfield in a city, Wright Field in Dayton, Ohio, as the Air Force's principal test facility. In the security-conscious late 1940s, Muroc (from which people commute to work, today, in Los Angeles) was distant and remote from prying eyes. In the parched heat above the cracked surface of the desert, a special breed of men, some with the right stuff, some not, kept pushing back the envelope. Muroc was where Captain Charles E Yeager had exceeded the speed of sound on 27 October 1947 in the Bell XS-1 rocket plane. Muroc was also where Captain Glen W Edwards was killed on 5 June 1948 in the crack-up of the Northrop YB-49 flying wing bomber, a loss which resulted in orders dated 8 December 1949 and a ceremony on 27 January 1950 applying the captain's name to Muroc and making it Edwards Air Force Base.

And it was here that the XF-88 came. Over 15–26 March 1949, Phase II testing was conducted by AMC on the number one airframe in seventeen flights totalling 17 hours, 57 minutes.

The number two airplane (46-526), although photographed with wingtanks on an earlier date, was officially rolled out on about 1 April 1949. It was different enough to warrant a change in designation from XF-88 to XF-88A. The XF-88A had two 4,100-lb (1859-kg) thrust Westinghouse J34-W E-15 engines. It had perforated rather than solid air brakes. But the most noticeable change was the extension to the exhaust tailpipe—the MAC 'short' afterburner.

## Afterburner

Bud Flesh: 'A year or so after the project had begun, we realized the need for, and the possibility of, getting better takeoff, climb and high speed performance with thrust augmentation such as some form of liquid injection or afterburning. It was concluded that afterburning would be more advantageous than liquid injection, at least as applied to this particular airplane. Accordingly, we approached

*After its arrival at Muroc Dry Lake, California, the XF-88 (46-525) works out on the California flatland. Underpowered performance with J34 engines later led to McDonnell being the first airframe manufacturer to design an afterburner for its own airplane, retrofitted to the number one XF-88 long after this March 1949 photo (MDC)*

RIGHT
*Unearthed by researcher Fred Roos, this March 1949 view shows the number one XF-88 on an early flight over Muroc Dry Lake and depicts the 'backwards' operation of the speed brakes. This innovative feature proved unsatisfactory in the flight test programme and more conventional speed brakes were later employed on XF-88 and F-101 aircraft (MDC)*

several engine and component manufacturers with a proposal that they develop an afterburner suitable for the J34 engine as installed in the XF-88. We specified that the maximum length not be more than 52 inches (1.3 m) since the airplane configuration, which was solidly frozen by that time, did not provide enough ground clearance for more.

'It was found, however, that all the [engine] manufacturers approached felt either that there was an inadequate market for another afterburner at that point except for the fact that we had been doing some combustion work of our own in connection with ram jets and pulse jets for helicopters, and felt that we might be able to assume the responsibility ourselves. We [did] not think it particularly appropriate for an airframe manufacturer to design and build afterburners, but experience with the overall installation made an airframe manufacturer more conscious than others of certain important requirements such as smooth external airflow with all positions of the nozzle.

'We had no test facilities of our own but were able to arrange for testing at the engine manufacturer's plant and in a Banshee in flight. We felt justified in this case in flying with a minimum of prior ground testing because we were using a two-engine airplane and could first install the afterburner on one side only, so that if it should fail, the pilot could still get home with reasonable safety.

'In developing this afterburner, we had five objectives: short length, good combustion efficiency, low internal drag or cold loss, low external drag, and high nozzle efficiency. These were accomplished primarily through two innovations. First, a unique combination diffuser and second, an iris nozzle. [The latter was] the first iris, or multiple-element nozzle successfully used with a turbojet engine.'

## XF-88A

The number two airplane, the XF-88A (46-526), first flew at St Louis on 26 April 1949. On 12 May 1949, at Muroc on its 70th flight, the number one XF-88 with Edholm presiding reached Mach 1.18 in a full 90-degree dive with military power. Edholm noted that, 'no buffeting or any other adverse condition whatever was encountered. The dive went from 42,000 ft (12,801 m) to 17,000 ft (5181 m) and the XF-88 was pointed straight down at 32,000 ft (9753 m) when clocked at 768 mph (1236 km/h). Maximum G force encountered was 3.4G in the recovery.' Bob Edholm was now among the few who'd travelled beyond the sound barrier.

Small wonder, then, that McDonnell expected to sell the Air Force squadrons of production F-88s which would be powered by 5,920-lb (2685-kg) thrust Westinghouse J46-WE-2 engines, and still employing the MAC short afterburner which *had* to be short because of clearance when the aircraft rotated. The F-88 Voodoo seemed the wave of the future. MAC salesmen could remind the Air Force that the XF-88 airplanes already had:

1. Dived past the speed of sound without exhibiting any buffet or limiting condition of any kind.

2. Exceeded the world's speed record by over 20 mph (36 km/h).

3. Exhibited excellent handling characteristics throughout the entire speed range.

Reams of material were being assembled by MAC people to try to persuade the Air Force that it needed the F-88 in its operational inventory. On 20 May 1949, production design layouts, preliminary tool design and production planning for F-88 airplanes was completed and submitted to AMC. This was done at MAC expense and the tab was $146,000. On 7 June 1949, the company made an informal proposal at AMC request for production of 50 F-88 aircraft at the rate of five per month. On 9 June 1949, flight tests of the afterburner were begun for the first time.

It may have been a little too late for the F-88, on the terms that existed in 1949. The US Air Force was already equipping with F-80 Shooting Stars and F-84 Thunderjets and was soon to have its first squadron of F-86A Sabres, which had the performance advantages of sweptwing technology but none of the drawbacks created by the F-88's requirement for massive fuel. Throughout 1949, work on the F-88 programme continued and various proposals were submitted for production of differing numbers of the new airplane. On 1 August 1949, at the request of AMC, a proposal for quantities of 42, 60, 80 and 108 F-88 penetration fighters with options for photo-reconnaissance airplanes was submitted to AMC's procurement division. The proposal called for a production rate of fifteen airframes per month.

The sales effort was getting nowhere. On 26 August 1949, the number one airplane was removed from flight status to conserve funds after completing 90 flights for a total of 79 hours and 3 minutes. On 23 October 1949, the number one XF-88 was placed in standby storage status. On 9 November, the number two XF-88A made an emergency landing at Muroc causing some damage and on 2 December, operations at Muroc were temporarily suspended. While the McDonnell team had been developing and flying their airplane, policymakers and politicians had been dreaming up a fly-off competition.

It had to be a time of disappointment for Ken Perkins, Bud Flesh, Bob Edholm and the hundreds of other people who had put so much of their lives into developing the F-88 at St Louis and Muroc. McDonnell had made a bold decision to forge ahead in 1949 when no information was available as to when any procurement action might be taken—believing in its airplane and trusting that since the F-88 was so outstanding, it made sense to further develop the design in advance of Phase II flight tests. The company had sunk not merely its wealth but its heart into developing its proposal for the production J46-

*In January 1949 at St Louis, months before its official
roll-out, XF-88A Voodoo 46-526 is seen with the 350-gal
wingtip tanks which were an inherent part of the fighter's
design from the beginning. Voodoo, with a nose pitot probe
which was later deleted, appears to have been allowed
outdoors solely to be photographed with wing tanks.
Airframe is not yet complete and national insignia have not
yet been applied
(MDC)*

powered aircraft. The airplane had met every test. The requirement that it compete with the XF-90 and YF-93A, imposed after most of those tests had been completed, was not merely a letdown. It was a slap in the face.

## Fly-Off Competition

Events moved ahead. On 20 March 1950, operations at the recently-renamed Edwards Air Force Base resumed as McDonnell people sought to prepare the XF-88 airplanes for the Air Force evaluation. The number two XF-88A, which had been brought back to St Louis, made the first flight since its emergency landing on 27 March and was ferried back to Edwards over 12–14 April.

The McDonnell people felt that they had long ago won an Air Force production order on sheer merit. Now instead of gearing up to produce squadrons of F-88s, they had to go up against two other aircraft types.

The Lockheed XF-90, developed by Clarence L (Kelly) Johnson's Burbank, California fighter team was nearly a year behind the MAC product, having made its first flight at Muroc on 6 June 1949. It was going through a similar flight-test regime. Indeed, the XF-90 had followed a similar course of development, with only the second of two prototypes (46-687/688) having afterburners. Powered by two 4,500-lb (2041-kg) thrust Westinghouse J34-W-11 turbojets and possessed of uncommonly graceful

*Readily visible here is the variable-position stabilator employed by the XF-88A Voodoo (46-526)* (MDC)

RIGHT
*Near the end of its active flying life on 4 August 1950, the XF-88A Voodoo (46-526) has a different nose pitot tube. The aircraft displays wing fences and perforated speed brakes which open in the opposite of the direction which would be expected* (MDC)

lines, the XF-90 had several advantages over the McDonnell aircraft, including the fact that it was stressed for up to 12Gs, while the Voodoo was limited to 6.5Gs. The XF-90 was dived through the sound barrier at Edwards on 17 May 1950 by company pilot Tony LeVier, reaching Mach 1.12.

The North American YF-93A was a latecomer to the three-way penetration fighter fly-off, first flown no earlier than 24 January 1950 with George Welch as pilot. Originally designated F-86C, and with no justifiable reason for its 'Y' service-test prefix, the YF-93A was an attempt to modify the F-86 Sabre for increased fuel capacity and endurance. It was the only one of the three competing designs with a single engine, the bulky 6,250-lb (2835-kg) thrust Pratt & Whitney J48-P-1 with afterburner. Two were built (47-317/318). Though the YF-93A came later and had the presumed benefit of the Sabre bloodline, from the beginning it was the least likely of the trio to succeed.

46

Over the period 17 April–18 May 1950, while gearing up for the actual flight competition to come the following month, the XF-88A and its six 20-mm cannons underwent preliminary armament flight testing at Edwards. This programme involved nine flights with 7.5 hours flying time. 4,261 rounds of 20-mm ammunition and 16 five-inch rockets were fired. Four 1,000-lb (454-kg) bombs were dropped. Surviving pictures of the XF-88A Voodoo as a bomber releasing ordnance over the California desert give a wholly different 'feel' for the airplane. Meanwhile on 1 May 1950, the number one airplane which had been returned to St Louis finally flew with belatedly-installed afterburners. Also that spring of 1950, the North Koreans were busily making plans.

It has been pointed out that ease of maintenance, in addition to flight performance, was to be an important part of the competition. McDonnell's team felt it was in good shape here.

*North American YF-93A (48-317), originally known as F-86C, in flight over Muroc Dry Lake with pilot George Welch at the controls. Last of the penetration fighter trio which also comprised the McDonnell XF-88 and Lockheed XF-90, this offshoot of the otherwise highly successful Sabre design was also the 'least best' of the three airplanes (NAA)*

RIGHT
*This Lockheed XF-90 (46-687), seen near Muroc, was one of two prototypes built. Despite graceful lines, the XF-90 was underpowered and came in second, behind the XF-88A Voodoo, in the 1950 penetration fighter competition. When Secretary of Defense James V Forrestal returned from a 1950 European survey with new plans to shift greater US emphasis to the use of atomic weapons, the need for any penetration fighter became questionable (Lockheed)*

On 11 May 1950, McDonnell submitted to Air Materiel Command yet another proposal for production of the F-88 aircraft. The proposal was for 28 airplanes plus a static-test vehicle based on 1951 procurement funds with delivery of the first airplane in May 1952 and a follow-up order of 150 airplanes out of 1952 procurement, the last 20 to be delivered in October 1953. It was the latest of many, many attempts over many years to sell an airplane which kept proving itself again and again. The penetration fighter fly-off competition hadn't been held yet, and AMC couldn't act until it had. And no one had asked North Korea's reckless, unpredictable leader, Kim Il-song.

## Fly-Off

On 22 May 1950, now with burners, airplane number one returned to Edwards to join its mate. With what seemed hundreds of millions of dollars at stake, men and machine convened on the California desert for the penetration fighter evaluation. Then, on its eve, after years of preparation, McDonnell suffered a

*By the time the first aircraft was photographed at St Louis in August 1950, 'short' afterburners had been added, changing the airplane's designation from XF-88 to XF-88A*
(MDC)

RIGHT
*In its entire career, the XF-88A Voodoo dropped only four bombs, in tests at Edwards AFB. Here, the aircraft carries two 1,000 lb (454 kg) iron bombs and six 5-in high-velocity aircraft rockets (HVAR). Further air-to-ground tests of the XF-88A were almost certainly cut short by budgetary constraints at a time when the Korean War established other priorities*
(MDC)

setback. On 16 June 1950, Major Frank K (Pete) Everest Jr made a wheels-up landing of the number two XF-88A following failure of an engine compressor. The evaluation would take place without Voodoo two.

Over the period 29 June–7 July 1950, while Americans read in their newspapers and heard on their radios of their soldiers being overwhelmed on a far away Asian peninsula, the penetration fighter evaluation was carried out. For fighter jocks at Edwards, it was an unparalleled opportunity to try out the newest and latest. One of the pilots was Lt Col Donald Blakeslee, wartime commander of the Mustang-equipped 4th Fighter Group and one of several World War 2 aces accompanying the Voodoo into the jet age. Another was Lt Col Walker (Bud) Mahurin, Thunderbolt ace with the 56th Fighter Group and soon to become a prisoner of war in Korea. Brigadier General Albert G Boyd, Lt Col Fred J Ascani and Major Everest tested all three aircraft types. Other practitioners of the right stuff who evaluated the XF-88A, XF-90 and YF-93A included Lt Col Dunham, Capt Gibson, Major

Butcher, Capt Aust and Major Rodeald. Others were Capt Murray, Lt Scol Schafter, Capt McLaughlin, Capt Newman and Major Johnson.

Thirty-six years later, retired Major General Fred J Ascani would regret that he had never been a collector of memorabilia or kept a diary. 'As the Director of Flight Test, I was obviously involved in the evaluation and flew all the candidate aircraft. Each aircraft had its advantages and disadvantages but, as I recall, the XF-90 and YF-93A were deficient in range. McDonnell's candidate, the XF-88, was clearly superior in this respect.' Ascani recalls that Major Charles E (Chuck) Yeager also flew the three fighters.

And few of them there are! Very little has survived on the historical record of those ten days on the California desert, coinciding as they did with defeat and retreat in Korea, when more than two dozen Air Force officers tried their hands on the fighter they might have to take to war. Few may remember now, but it was a devastating blow to national pride when the infantrymen of Task Force Smith were overrun by North Korean troops using Soviet T-34 tanks at

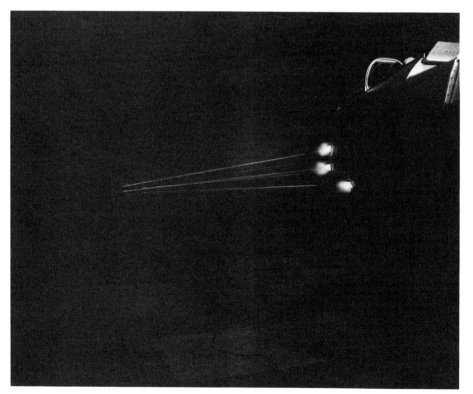

To test the gun installation for the XF-88 Voodoo McDonnell built this nose mockup installation which carried six M39 20 mm cannons intended for the fighter (MDC)

LEFT
On 2 March 1949, the nose mockup installation of the XF-88 Voodoo unleashes a powerful stream of gunfire from its six 20 mm M39 cannons (MDC)

Suwon, and the communists appeared to be driving for the sea. The test pilots at Edwards received hourly reminders, via the news, that the US Air Force's next fighter aircraft would have to not merely fly but fight. The MiG-15 was *still* unknown in the West—*that* surprise would come with China's entry into the war in November—but in June at Edwards, the mood can hardly have been cheerful. It is not recorded whether the men compared XF-88, XF-90 and YF-93A over Tecate Beer at Pancho Barnes' Fly Inn bar and restaurant at the edge of Rodgers Dry Lake.

As it turned out, the fly-off competition might as well not have been held at all!

It can hardly have surprised many people that the XF-88 Voodoo won the competition. Proponents of the Voodoo had felt that it was 'no contest' from the beginning.

What *was* a surprise, what hurt—profoundly, deeply—was that it didn't *help* to win the contest.

'We couldn't believe it,' says an official associated with the XF-88 programme who shall remain unnamed. 'We had beaten the pants off the competition, fair and square. We had a fighter that everybody *knew* was the *perfect* fighter for the Air Force. And just a few months later, the MiG-15 appeared in Korea and the Air Force had to hurriedly rush over a few F-86A Sabres to cope with it. We could have had F-88s in combat in Korea.'

What seems to have happened is that priorities changed. No one had ever pretended that the Voodoo was an interceptor (although a proposal for an interceptor version *did* exist, and the F-101B later proved effective in that role), and the Air Force seems to have decided—Korea or no Korea—to place greater emphasis on preparing to cope with the Soviet bomber threat. Funds which might have been committed to the Voodoo went instead to F-86D, F-89D and F-94A interceptors for the Air Defense Command (ADC) which, by the mid-fifties, would have as many as five dozen fighter squadrons defending North America.

Air Material Command (AMC), headquartered at Wright-Patterson AFB, Ohio, waited until 11 September 1950 to deliver the bad news in the form of a letter from one Orval R Cook, who enjoyed the title Director, Procurement and Industrial Planning and whose rank is given in the same letter as both brigadier general and major general. Cook did not sign above his own name in any event, the letter being signed for him by one Phillip W Smith. Addressed to McDonnell and referring to two earlier communications (letters written in May 1950), the 'Cook Letter' was a classic example of good news, bad news:

'... *The McDonnell XF-88 was ranked no. 1 of three aircraft evaluated. No procurement of any of the three aircraft types evaluated is contemplated at this time.*

As a jet-propelled fighter to equip squadrons and kill MiGs, the F-88 Voodoo was dead. There was, however, another future awaiting the aircraft type—one which involved propellers.

## XF-88B

Going back to 25 July 1949 when McDonnell received Air Force contract AF33 (038)-7442, plans were underway to convert the first XF-88 Voodoo (46-525) into a research testbed for high-speed propellers.

The 2,500 shp Allison T38, or company Model 501 F-1, turboprop engine was to be installed in the nose in addition to the Westinghouse J34 turbojets already fitted. Propeller gearbox ratios would provide three prop speeds, 1700, 3600 and 6000 rpm. The aircraft would be compatible with propellers of 4-, 7- and 10 feet (1.2-, 2.1- and 3.0 metres).

After extensive studies and numerous changes, the number one XF-88 airframe, which as noted had already been brought up to XF-88A standard with the addition of MAC short afterburners, was modified for the propeller testbed role as the XF-88B during the period August through November 1952. The first ground run of the newly installed XT38, for 29 minutes, was on 16 February 1953.

The July 1953 issue of McDonnell's house organ, *Airscoop*, announced flight tests of the XF-88B as a project of the Propeller Laboratory of the Air Force's Air Research and Development Central (ARDC), as the Air Materiel Command had now been re-named, with cooperation from the US Navy's Bureau of Aeronautics and the National Advisory Committee for Aeronautics (NACA). Until then, the 14 April 1953 first flight of the XF-88B at St Louis had not been revealed. Remarkably, with the 10-ft (3.4-m) prop, ground clearance was a scant 6.7 inches. The XF-88B was designed to take off with the prop feathered, a sight the designer, Bud Flesh, always found 'incredible.' At high altitude, the turboprop engine would be started for brief test runs of 20 minutes or so during which time powerplant and propeller would be monitored and evaluated.

McDonnell pilots made 16 test flights in the XF-88B, concluding on 16 June 1953. The first flight by an Air Force pilot was made on 23 June 1953.

The NACA supersonic propeller programme was intended to explore the design and practicality of propellers for economic propulsion of aircraft—to cruise at Mach numbers up to 0.95. NACA wanted a B-45 or B-47 bomber as a testbed, but the XF-88B became the choice. After acceptance, the XF-88B was flown by Captain John Fitzpatrick to Langley with a stopover at Wright-Patterson AFB where it was flown by other Air Force pilots before arriving at Langley AFB, Virginia, on 13 July 1953. Langley is in the heavily-populated Virginia region known as the tidewater and is one of the oldest American military airfields. Testing of various propeller configurations got under way at this historic airbase with NACA project pilots John P (Jack) Reeder and William L Alford doing the flying. Alford was later killed in a Blackburn Buccaneer crash in Britain in 1959. And Reeder? Says a co-worker, 'To me he is one of the honest-to-goodness living legends in test

**TOP LEFT**
*XF-88B taking off in the usual manner with its propeller feathered. This view from beneath illustrates the difficulty that went into re-designing the aircraft to accommodate both the turboprop engine and the nose landing gear (MDC)*

**LEFT**
*With St Louis' Mississippi River in background, XF-88B Voodoo is pictured before delivery to NACA. Most in-flight photos of the XF-88B testbed showed the propeller at a standstill as the aircraft flew on jet power only (MDC)*

**ABOVE**
*The XF-88B, serial 46-525, was operated by NACA from 13 July 1953 to 16 September 1958. At the NACA acceptance ceremony in July 1953 are (left to right) John P (Jack) Reeder, chief of flight operations for the NACA test programme; Jerry Hammack, project engineer for NACA's supersonic propeller programme; Capt John Fitzpatrick, project test pilot; Art Voheley, engineer; William L Alford, NACA test pilot; Jack King, flight test engineer, and Gene Smith, project crewchief (Reeder)*

flying.' A third NACA pilot, Bob Sommers, is thought to have had some experience with the Voodoo—if not the XF-88B, then the F-101A.

The pure-jet XF-88A (46-526) arrived at Langley AFB very shortly after the XF-88B, with 317:55 hours on its airframe—and never flew again. The XF-88A, incidentally, had an all-moving horizontal tail in contrast to the fixed stabilizer and elevator of the XF-88B. NACA lacked the resources to fly both airframes, if indeed it ever had intended to fly 46-526 as a 'control' for comparison purposes, so the number two machine was used for spare J34 engine and airframe parts. This fine airplane was rapidly cannibalized and transformed into a gutted skeleton of its former self.

Some aspects of the XF-88B turboprop flight programme seemed odd. With three engines using fuel from the same tanks, the XF-88B had to be towed to runway's end before takeoff to conserve fuel. Jack Reeder made flight number one on 30 June 1953,

testing turboprop power with various control surfaces and encountering some oscillation. He was operating a 10-ft (3-m) propeller at 1700 rpm. At one point, the oscillation caused him to feather the prop. In flight number two, also on 30 June 1953, Reeder started the T38 engine at 20,000 ft (6096 m). His notes on these and on flight number three, 1 July 1953, indicated difficulty landing after the turboprop evaluation segment of the flight was finished.

No fewer than eleven propellers were planned for flight-test on the XF-88B but only three were actually flown, each with a distinctively different prop spinner hub, including one which resembled a turnip. As McDonnell historian Dick Powers points out, very little information about these tests has survived. To jump ahead of the story, NACA also acquired two F-101A Voodoos, 53-2434 which was ferried from Edwards to Langley by Jack Reeder on 22 August 1956, and 54-1442 received by NACA on 18 April 1958. Reeder notes that very little was done with the

former aircraft. 53-2434 ended its flying days when ferried to Davis-Monthan AFB, Arizona, on 1 March 1960 with 236:55 hours on the airframe; 54-1442 had had 168:10 hours on the airframe when it reached NACA and departed on 22 December 1958 with 184:40. Why only 14 hours of flying? Explains Reeder, 'They were to be used by [NACA's] Langley Research Center for research on the integration of high performance airframe, target acquisition, tracking systems and weaponry. However, when we became NASA [National Aeronautics and Space Administration] in 1958 [after the Soviet satellite Sputnik focussed attention on outer space], programmes involving the F-101As were cancelled. In performing research for this narrative, NASA's Robert L Burns learned that several of the Langley Research Center photo negatives of XF-88A, XF-88B and the two F-101As had, by 1986, been cracked and spoilt because of age, inattention, or both.

The XF-88B arrived at Langley with 146:36 hours

*Sunlight study of the XF-88B Voodoo aircraft after delivery to NACA at Langley AFB, Virginia. The airframe was eventually allowed to rot in a dump at Langley, together with its pure-jet XF-88A counterpart. Ironically, the XF-88B may have helped to prove that turboprop power, of the sort envisaged for the US Navy's Douglas A2D-1 Skyshark attack plane, was not a practical substitute for pure jet powerplants* (Reeder)

on its airframe and completed the turboprop test programme with 174:24. It made 43 research flights. Its last flight was on 17 January 1958. Reeder considered its role as a turboprop testbed 'strictly marginal.'

At one time, when both airframes glinted in the sunshine, somebody pointed at them and asked what they were. There were fewer aviation publications in the 1950s, and not everyone had even heard of the XF-88s. An Air Force officer provided the explanation. 'Them planes over there are a couple of big silver orphans. Seems like nobody don't want them for nothing. They could have made a right nice fighter, too.'

If some sort of penalty ought to be set aside for whoever kept the F-88 Voodoo from entering production, the lowest level of hades ought to be reserved for the Langley AFB official who ordered the two Voodoo airframes scrapped. The XF-88A (46-526) was turned over to Langley AFB base salvage on 7 July 1958 and the XF-88B followed on 16 September 1958. The first-named had already become more a mishmash collection of spare parts than an actual airplane. Aviation enthusiasts who

were active in the late 1950s, including the author, Merle Olmsted and Gary Kuhn, have vivid memories of the two Voodoos sitting in the dump—forlorn, desolate. There were fewer aviation museums in the 1950s, too, and despite the many years that had gone into the design and creation of the two F-88s, no way could be found to preserve them. After several years in the dump, the two Voodoos were dismantled. They exist today only in the many pictures that were taken of them between 1948 and 1960.

## Defeat

Failure to reward effort can produce a range of results. In later years, busy people who labour under pressure would speak of burnout. The Air Force's decision to cancel the XF-88 contract has been attributed to other reasons in addition to those already cited, including a shortage of funds that had been forewarned by President Harry S Truman as far back as 1948 and to increased expenditure on the B-36, one of the bombers that the F-88 had been designed to escort. Furthermore, a significant number of Republic F-84E Thunderjets, under

contract since late 1948, had already entered the Air Force inventory and could satisfy immediate requirements for a penetration fighter. The F-84G variant did, in fact, become widely used in SAC. The interceptor version of the now-proven North American Sabre, the F-86D, had made its first flight on 22 December 1949 with Joseph Lynch at the controls and seemed, at the time, the best of several candidates to meet the urgent requirements for a better interceptor.

Even with the F-84G and the sweptwing F-84F entering service in SAC's strategic fighter squadrons, SAC's own top brass were not fully satisfied and still wanted a Voodoo-like fighter capable of escorting the transoceanic B-36s. It is often forgotten how long General Curtis E LeMay reigned over the Strategic Air Command—from 16 October 1948 to 30 June 1957—and while LeMay was far from a fighter advocate in many contexts, he *did* want SAC to have a bigger, farther-ranging fighter. On 12 January 1951, SAC outlined the minimum characteristics needed in a new penetration/escort fighter known to be brought into service on an interim basis over the period 1952–1953. SAC's fighters would serve with units

*The end—for now. Forlorn and desolate, XF-88A Voodoo 46-526 rots in the scrap heap at Langley AFB, Virginia, in 1959. XF-88B airplane 46-525 suffered a similar fate in the same place, both airplanes being scrapped eventually. But the Voodoo design still had a future.*
*(Robert F Dorr)*

LEFT
*One of the more unusual views of one of the lesser-known nose configurations of the XF-88B Voodoo turboprop test bed, at the NACA facility at Langley AFB, Virginia. Sensors extending horizontally from the fuselage side measured the performance of the propeller when it turned at supersonic speeds*
*(Reeder)*

known as Strategic Fighter Wings (SFW), to distinguish them from the Fighter-Bomber Wings (FBW) of Tactical Air Command and the Fighter-Interceptor Wings (FIW) of Air Defense Command.

The January 1951 requirement offered a glimmer of hope to the demoralized people at McDonnell who had worked so hard on the F-88, who *believed* in their airplane, and who wanted to succeed. Although McDonnell had failed to sell the F-88, it had now spent half a decade putting together a first-class fighter team to meet the follow-on 6 February 1951 General Operational Requirement (GOR), which was later called Skeleton GOR 101 and subsequently expanded as GOR 101-2. In St Louis, it was the beginning of a fighter dynasty, company chief James McDonnell and his nephew Sanford (Sandy) McDonnell being well-placed to direct the efforts of top-calibre people like designer Bud Flesh in addressing the new SAC requirement. The machine they would produce was Flesh's design. It would be known as the Manufacturers Model 36W and—under the Pentagon's integrated, 'systems' approach of procurement—as Weapon System 105A before men started calling it by its right name, which was F-101 Voodoo.

At the beginning of 1951, defeat was the only word to characterize the efforts of the McDonnell Aircraft Company to sell a fighter to the Air Force. But the company was unknown no longer. The F2H-2 and F2H-2P Banshee were to become the first of its products to see combat—in Korea, where fighting would continue to rage until the 27 July 1953 armistice. The F2H-3 and F2H-4 Banshee, the 'long' variants of the straightwing fighter often named the Banjo, were bulwarks of the US Navy and Marine Corps in the 1950s. The F3H-1 Demon was coming along. It may not have been a fighter dynasty quite yet, and the giants in the fighter field were still Lockheed, Northrop and North American, but the feisty McDonnell firm was going to be heard from again. In February 1951, engineer Melvin Pobre looked at Flesh, reminded him that SAC was still knocking on the door, and waxed philosophical. 'We've taken it on the chin for a long time, but we're going to make it with a new Voodoo.' Pobre screwed his face into an exaggerated 'fair is fair' expression and added:

'By golly, we're gonna make a fighter for the Air Force!'

*By February 1952, when the two XF-88 airframes were caught together at the St Louis plant with some sleek, Korean War-era Fords, Chevys and Hudsons in the background, there was no longer any prospect of a production order. By this time, both aircraft have MAC 'short' afterburners and are designated XF-88A. Only the second machine, in foreground, is armed with cannons (MDC)*

# Chapter 3
# The Case for the Escort Fighter
## Bringing the F-101A Into Service

By late 1950, it seemed more certain than ever that politics and purse-strings would betray the labour, love, and thousands of manhours that went into the F-88 Voodoo, including work on the production F-88 which would have been longer and larger than the prototypes. But the January 1951 SAC requirement kept alive the concept of a twin-engine escort fighter. Among ideas put forth by McDonnell's fighter team were a company-initiated proposal for a new machine to be powered by Allison J71 engines and a design to fit an Air Force counter-proposal for twin Pratt & Whitney J57s.

The designation F-101, second in the 'century' series, was allocated in November 1951 at a time when Americans believed the Korean War would end soon and the top brass were concerned about the US-Soviet standoff. The Strategic Air Command retained its pre-eminence within the Air Force, and amid decisions about procurement some generals and admirals wallowed shamelessly in the inter-service rivalry of the period. Others believed with justification and argued honourably that the escort fighter for SAC was needed now, for the MiG-15 had shown the danger of presuming Soviet technology to be second-rate. A teenaged Civil Air Patrol cadet argued for the F-101 in *Air Force* magazine under the title, 'The Case for the Escort Fighter.' 14-year-old Robert F Dorr's first paid magazine piece failed to set the world afire, but it was a time when MAC, ARDC and SAC *wanted* the F-101 Voodoo. And what SAC wanted, SAC got.

It was mockup time again. Edward M (Bud) Flesh, designer of the F-101, describes this vital step in the development process:

'Before the actual design of the F-101 started, the first thing we had to do was to create a mockup. A mockup is a wooden replica [which] shows where the various equipment is located, armament, electronics, cockpit configuration, etc. It also shows access to this

equipment. When it is finished a group of Air Force representatives from the various departments at Wright Field, some 20 to 25 people, come to the plant to inspect the mockup. The cockpit configuration usually gets the most attention. A group of pilots get together and rearrange the cockpit to their satisfaction including the instrument panel. The mockup is complete with lighting, so they can judge the ease of reading the instruments at night.

'While the [F-101A] mockup was being built, wind-tunnel models were also being built. Low speed tunnel models and supersonic tunnel models were made and tested. From these tests the aerodynamics people decided to move the horizontal stabilizer up high on the vertical fin.

'Early in 1952, we started to build up our F-101A project.' The top men at MAC included John Aldridge, who became Vice President for Marketing, Robert V Coleman, Project Flight Test Engineer, Wayne Lowe, equipment engineer, Dick Noyes, later project engineer for the F-101B, Jim Schaff, administrative engineer, Ray Pepping, structural dynamics engineer, and Charles Beard, photographic expert and project engineer of the RF-101A/C. 'The organization was simple at first,' continues Flesh's recollection, 'consisting of a project leader for each specialty, such as structures, landing gear, hydraulics, electrical, electronics, cockpit, engine and installation. The group built up to approximately 250 people and design drawings began to pour into the shop.

'Meanwhile, Pratt & Whitney was testing and perfecting the J57-P-13 engine which we had chosen. They designed and built afterburners for the engine.

'We devoted the entire fuselage aft of the cockpit to fuel tanks in order to carry 2,341 gals. Internally, we had five tanks arranged longitudinally along the fuselage. If we used fuel out of an after tank until it was empty, the airplane would be badly out of

balance. Likewise, if we fed out of # 1 tank toward, the same case. Therefore we installed fuel control valves in each tank, which drained fuel out of each tank alternately, keeping the airplane in balance. When external tanks were used, the 450 gals in a single tank were used first and the tank was dropped.'

Flesh notes that long hours and a lot of overtime work went into the design period. 'We used an integrated type of construction for the major bulkheads. They were hugged out of big aluminum pressings instead of being built out of sheet metal and extrusions. Sheet metal webs in the engine section were made out of titanium to withstand the heat.

'Due to the longer length of the fuselage ahead of the ducts, it was thought advisable to include a boundary layer bleed at the inboard side of the engine ducts.'

*Final assembly of the first F-101A Voodoo (53-2418) in the McDonnell St Louis plant in August 1954, a month before its first flight. The words* McDonnell Voodoo *were later moved from tail to nose and the highlighting of the tail number was removed. Note air brakes in extended position*
*(MDC)*

63

## Rollout

Assembly of the major units of the first F-101A Voodoo (53-2418) was completed at the St Louis plant on 20 August 1954. The new fighter was rolled into the sunshine for 'photo sessions' with some of the people who would have key roles in the flight test programme, including Flesh and chief test pilot Robert C Little. Also present was James S McDonnell. McDonnell had always said that his firm was not going to remain small and that his products would prove themselves, and the F-101A Voodoo was going to do both.

The Voodoo's twin J57-P-13 turbojets were rated at 10,200-lb (4627 kg) thrust, which increased to 15,000 lb (6804 kg) with afterburning. Armed with four 20-mm M39 cannon, it was supposed to be

*F-101A Voodoo (53-2418) taking shape. Yet to fly in this August 1954 view in St Louis, this airframe has survived to the present day. The aircraft is at the aircraft museum at Pueblo Memorial Airport, Colorado, where director William Feder Sr invites assistance from anyone interested in helping with its restoration*
*(MDC)*

ABOVE RIGHT
*Early in the flight test programme for the F-101A Voodoo (53-2418), the prototype poses with its makers in St Louis. Left to right: E M (Bud) Flesh, project engineer, James S McDonnell, founder and chairman of the company bearing his name, and Bob Little, chief test pilot. As the overcoats suggest, it is November 1954*
*(MDC)*

capable of carrying a 1,620-lb (735-kg) or 3,721-lb (1688-kg) centreline nuclear weapon. The aircraft introduced an alphabet soup of new equipment items including the MB-1 cruise relief autopilot, ASN-6 (GPI) dead-reckoning navigation system, ARN-14 navigation radio, MA-7 fire-control system with all-weather radar and optical gunsighting, ASP-54 radar warning system, and the MA-2 low altitude bombing system.

Despite appearances, the F-101A was not yet a complete airplane. 53-2418 was an assembly of components which were quickly disassembled, loaded aboard two C-124 Globemaster transports, and carted out to the California desert. In later years, when McDonnell Aircraft Company became one of the largest and best-proven airplane manufacturers, a number of prototypes made their first flights in St

Louis. In 1954, the Voodoo's maiden flight was to occur at Edwards Air Force Base.

The F-101A was the heaviest single-seat fighter ever built. It went to the desert to push back the envelope. In 1954, 'century series' meant the latest, the best, the hottest aircraft to be flown by the best pilots at the farthest reaches.

Robert C Little had flown P-51 Mustangs in World War 2. After a brief gap when Bob Edholm went off flying in February 1952, Little became MAC chief test pilot. He prepared himself diligently for the first flight in the F-101A, a plane which no pilot would ever say was easy to fly. Bob Little's personal notes on the first flight of the first Voodoo for this volume:

'The first flight was made on 29 September 1954. It was a very dramatic flight. Without question, the F-101A at the time had the highest thrust to weight ratio

First flight
29 Sept 1954
Edwards AFB

Bob Little

*F-101A Voodoo (53-2418), progenitor of 807 airframes to follow, on the North Lake Bed at Muroc Dry Lake, California, in September 1954, immediately prior to its first flight. The F-101A had made its first 'flight' in pieces aboard two C-124 Globemasters from St Louis to Edwards AFB shortly before this sunlit view*
*(MDC)*

LEFT
*Robert C Little, McDonnell's chief test pilot, grins at project engineer Edward M (Bud) Flesh on the occasion of the first flight of the F-101A Voodoo (52-3418) on 29 September 1054. Little exceeded Mach 1 on the maiden trip aloft, a feat he was not able to repeat when he flew the first F4H-1 Phantom a half-decade later*
*(MDC)*

and the highest wing loading of any fighter aircraft ever built. The performance on the initial takeoff and the remainder of the first flight was spectacular, to say the least, and the Voodoo at military power easily out-ran the F-100 chase plane in full afterburning. Also on the first flight a supersonic speed of 1.07 Mach number was achieved which was the first time any airplane had been flown supersonic on its initial flight. A number of engine stalls were encountered during the early flights, which required some adjustment to engine controls, plus a substantial redesign of the inlet.

'It was a maximum afterburner takeoff and I had the airplane defuelled to about 8,000 lbs internal. I let the T-33 camera plane call brake release when he

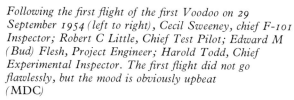

*Following the first flight of the first Voodoo on 29 September 1954 (left to right), Cecil Sweeney, chief F-101 Inspector; Robert C Little, Chief Test Pilot; Edward M (Bud) Flesh, Project Engineer; Harold Todd, Chief Experimental Inspector. The first flight did not go flawlessly, but the mood is obviously upbeat (MDC)*

ABOVE RIGHT
*A little-known chore of the very first Voodoo (53-2418) was to test the General Electric J79 engines used in the F-4 Phantom, as seen here in October 1958 only a few months after the Phantom's first flight. The programme is something of a historical mystery: numerous people closely associated with the nummber one airframe could not remember the J79 tests and did not know why they were conducted. It is unlikely the US Air Force ever saw the J79 as a powerplant for the operational Voodoo (MDC)*

thought he was in position to get movies. I told him earlier than things were going to move pretty fast, but he didn't really believe me. At any rate, no movies were obtained of the takeoff, since all he had was the rear view of a cloud of dust from the North Lake Bed at Edwards.

'The F-100 chase plane, even with a 350 knot [500 km/h] starting speed, was using his afterburner to stay anywhere close. The [F-101A] nose gear didn't retract immediately for no particular reason since on later afterburner takeoffs, it did. At any rate [on the first flight, the nose gear] retracted of its own accord at about 15,000 feet [4572 m] after I had come out afterburner.'

It is fanciful to imagine the scene: Little, pushing the F-101A Voodoo through dazzling sunshine, T-33 and F-100 unable to keep up!

'At about this time the engines started stalling at random intervals and this continued throughout the flight. Nevertheless, I climbed the airplane to 35,000 feet [9298 m] at military power, climbing at about .92 Mach number which was running the F-100 chase

plane out of fuel. I did numerous telemetered flutter checks and then went supersonic in a shallow let-down.' This is understood to be the first time any prototype aircraft went supersonic on its maiden voyage.

In a serious job demanding the right stuff, Little was not without humour. Recalls Flesh, 'Lockheed had the reputation of exaggerating the performance of their airplanes. Before the first flight, Bob Little, Bob Coleman, our flight test engineer, and others from our plant got together and wrote a script for a little skit in which we exaggerated beyond all reason the performance of the F-101A. Things like Bob saying it met all of its guarantees on the first flight. We rehearsed it, and did the skit for Colonel Arnold Phillips the Air Force Project Officer, who by the way was one swell guy. He recognized what we were doing, went along with us, then broke it up by saying, "Now, what *really* happened?"'

The Voodoo soared above the desert. Flesh remembers, 'Bob pushed it a little farther on the next flight and we ran into our first bit of trouble. At speeds near Mach 1, Bob put it into a tight turn and a loud bang occurred, frightening the hell out of the pilot. The airplane was still under control, but an engine was dead. At lower speed he got it started again and came on in. The Pratt & Whitney man diagnosed it as an engine stall and installed probes to measure air pressure at the face of the engine. We found that due to the curve in the duct we were getting uneven pressures at the face of the compressor. We corrected this problem by modifying the lips of the duct entrance, moving them forward slightly, and adding turning vanes in the duct.'

37 days after Little's first flight, Air Force evaluation of the F-101A Voodoo began in November 1954. Brigadier General J Stanley Holtner, head of Edwards' Air Force Flight Test Center (AFFTC) became the first Air Force general to go aloft in the Voodoo. Holtner gained this distinction apparently on 5 November 1954 in aircraft number three (53-2420).

Already, the Voodoo had teething troubles. Indeed, there seemed enough problems to raise doubt

*Final resting place for the prototype F-101A Voodoo (53-2418) is the Vintage Aircraft Display in Pueblo, Colorado, where the markings on the progenitor of the species appear inaccurate. Museum director William Feder Sr explains that the engines are missing, the Voodoo needs a lot of work, and volunteer assistance is needed to restore valuable airframes in the collection*
(Feder)

BELOW
*Brigadier General J Stanley Holtner, commander of the Air Force Flight Test Center (AFFTC) at Edwards AFB, Calif., had the distinction of being the first general to fly the Voodoo, on 5 November 1954. As chief of the USAF's principal test centre, Holtner flew various types including the F-86D Sabre (51-6168) in this previously unpublished 13 November 1953 picture*
(USAF)

whether SAC would ever receive the fighter which was being regarded less and less as an escort and more as a nuclear delivery platform.

As already noted, civilian and military pilots began encountering compressor stalls at high speed, a phenomenon which was to continue until considerable work was done on J57 engine and air intake ducts. Many McDonnell people claim that the bulk of this work was done by themselves rather than by the engine manufacturer. The three principal problems, however, were: (1) the Voodoo's tendency for the nose to pitch up at high angles of attack; (2) the undercarriage; and (3) the main horizontal control slab bellcrank.

## The Pitch-Up Problem

Bob Little is well aware of a notorious fault which caused some to argue that the Voodoo might never prove combat-ready—its pitch-up problem. The T-tail configuration of the F-101A was the cause: at high angles of attack the wing disrupted and blocked the airflow over the horizontal tail, causing it to lose lift, resulting in a severe nose pitch-up, sometimes followed by a potentially fatal spin.

Little will be quoted on this problem momentarily. Pitch-up will be a continuing ingredient in the narrative which follows. A good layman's explanation was provided for this volume by a fighter pilot of no small repute, Robin Olds. 'Watch it, buster!' Olds warns. 'It didn't take much to go into a pitch-up at altitude, even in cruise. Reason: the angle of attack needed to achieve lift at, let's say, 34 thousand [feet, 10,353 m] with full drops [droptanks] and internal fuel was awfully close to the pitch-up stall point, where the flow of air over the wings created a downflow over the slab, which the slab could not accommodate.' Olds points out that during air-to-air refuelling, there was always a marked contrast in angle of attack between KC-135A and F-101A, as the reader will shortly be reminded.

Bob Little says, 'On the early flights, there were no indications of pitch-up because the engines always stalled heavily during manoeuvring flight and you could not take the airplane to the pitch-up boundary. As I recall, it was about six months into the flight programme, after we had made some improvements to reduce engine stalls, that I got the first pitch-up which was in a windup turn at 1.2 Mach number testing for engine stalls. This manoeuvre documented the fact that the airplane would have pitch-up within the normal manoeuvring boundary and launched a long and torturous experimental programme relating to the alleviation of pitch-up.

'The first true pitch-up encountered in the F-101A was when I was doing a supersonic engine stall investigation during high altitude windup turns. This was probably in November of 1955, after we had made enough improvements on the engine and inlets that the engine stall boundary was higher than the

*Key figures in the F-101A Voodoo programme. Robert C Little (left), was chief test pilot on Voodoo and Phantom and is now senior vice president. James S McDonnell (centre), Chairman of McAir, founded and nurtured the fighter team which bears his name. John Aldridge (right) was Vice President for Marketing for McAir (MDC)*

pitch-up boundary. Up until this time, engine stalls had precluded full investigation of the manoeuvring boundary of the airplane. On the flight the pitch-up occurred I was at about 1.3 Mach number and 28,000 feet [8534 m] and it was quite a surprise. After that we launched a heavy programme to define and determine a fix for pitch-up.'

While Phase III tests on the Voodoo were unfolding and SAC pilots were starting to join the programme, the nasty pitch-up phenomenon apparently caused Captain John T Dolan to spin out of control in his F-101A and to lose his life on the California desert, apparently in Voodoo number two (52-4319). Can this be the same incident recalled by McDonnell's E F Peters? 'Before the spin programme and other actions solved what to do when the airplane pitched up, an Air Force captain rode the first airplane lost at Edwards almost to the ground. This airplane contacted the ground in a level position with zero ground speed. There were no skid marks and no evidence any part of the airplane touched the ground before the rest of it. There was a tall pole standing in the ground that was less than a yard from the fuselage, aft of the wing and forward of the stabilator, and it was untouched.' If Peters is right, this was simply one of those extraordinary events in aviation which make truth more bizarre than fiction.

The test programme was expanding, ordnance tests to be conducted by Air Proving Ground Command at Eglin AFB, Florida, but the pitch-up threat—although played down, at first, by the manufacturer—refused to go away. On 10 January 1956, Major Lonnie R Moore, a Korean War jet ace with ten MiG-15 kills, was taking off from Eglin when the nose of his aircraft pitched up and he went in. The death of the Korean War fighter ace made headlines and alerted the Pentagon brass that even an experienced pilot could have difficulty with what Colonel Allan Young calls, 'that great big, wonderful old bastard of an airplane.'

McDonnell engineers and Air Force systems people struggled mightily to find a solution for the pitch-up problem. The first F-101A Voodoos were to be delivered to SAC's 27th Strategic Fighter Wing at Bergstrom AFB, Texas, near Austin, but the Air Force was having second thoughts. Tests proved that it *was* possible to recover from pitch-up and from the resulting incipient spin by applying full nose-down stabilator and neutralizing rudder and ailerons—but it required plenty of altitude. If, like Major Moore, you were close to the ground when it happened, you were dead. To be sure, despite the Air Force's concern, experienced pilots believed that the airplane could be flown, even in combat, if the parameters of its flight envelope were respected.

A device called an active inhibitor, which was neither active nor inhibiting, was eventually developed to sound a warning klaxon for the pilot's benefit when pitch-up was about to occur. Pilots called the device a 'stick knocker' because it forced the stick forward, whether they liked it or not. The sensor for this device, which also illuminated a yellow light on the instrument panel, was located on the left side of the Voodoo's nose, below the cockpit.

The active pitch inhibitor resulted from the thorough review that had begun in May 1956. Meanwhile, some Pentagon people were noting that with its high dash speed and endurance, the Voodoo might be better suited for other roles— reconnaissance and interception—where the pitch-up problem would be less threatening than in air-to-air engagements with other fighters. More than a decade after the first steps were taken to design it, the Voodoo was still an airplane in search of a mission, still an orphan, a 'homeless waif' as one pilot put it. Amid some controversy—at least one McDonnell

*In January 1956, the much-worked F-101A Voodoo (53-2421), still wearing tufts from other tests, flew a much-heralded 'double header' refuelling mission, using the 'flying boom' method with this KC-97F (51-291) over St Louis and employing the 'probe and drogue' system for a second refuelling on the same flight over Wright Field. This was the first time the Voodoo had been refuelled in mid-air, a capability essential to its planned long-range escort role (MDC)*

TOP

*The number four F-101A Voodoo (52-3421) was a busy 'dog ship,' being submitted to spin tests and air-refuelling trials. First, however, Voodoo Four posed with B-47B Stratojet (51-2198), to illustrate the bombers it would escort. USAF's Air Materiel Command (AMC) has changed its name to Air Research and Development Command (ARDC) by this time and the Stratojet was borrowed for the St Louis photo session from ARDC's Wright Field, Ohio facility*
*(MDC)*

ABOVE

*Still busy as a beaver, fourth F-101A Voodoo (53-2421) by November 1956 has sprouted a lengthy and unusual tail housing for spin-test parachute apparatus. In foreground, F-101A Voodoo (53-2446) c/n 29 wears an Air Proving Ground Command (APGC) badge, suggesting this photo was taken at Eglin AFB, Florida*
*(MDC)*

Close-up of the tail extension retrofitted to F-101A Voodoo (53-2421) for spin trials, in November 1956, apparently at

Eglin and (below) 'cutaway' photo of the spin parachute in the tail section
(MDC)

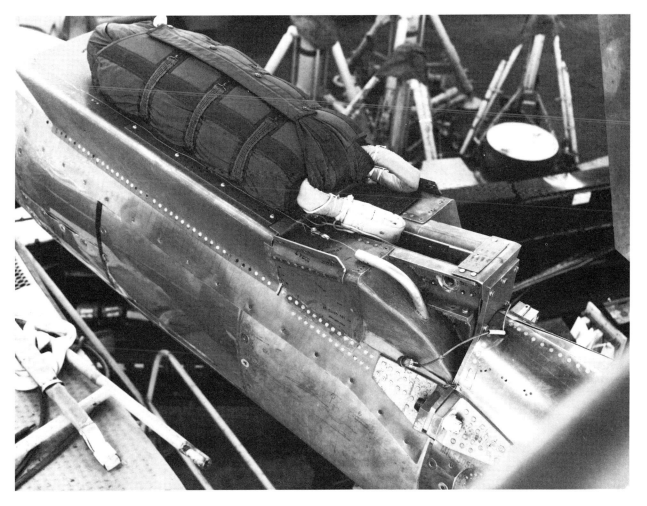

*Landing gear problems, of various kind, plagued the Voodoo throughout its career. An undercarriage failure lies behind this view of a cherry picker lifting the number nine F-101A Voodoo (53-2426) out of the mud and back onto the runway at St Louis in August 1955*

ABOVE RIGHT
*External stores tests for the F-101A were flown at Edwards AFB with ship number thirteen (53-2430). 22 flights from 29 August 1957 to 22 May 1958 totalled 26 hours, 30 minutes flying time. Because the F-101A was a single-seat aircraft, engineer Ken Carter could not go along and conducted the tests at a radio in the operations building. Telemetry was not used in 1957–58, and pilot Capt Swart H Nelson was often out of touch for worrying periods of time—but the tests succeeded routinely (both MDC)*

employee felt that the J46-powered F-88 design of six years earlier was a better airplane—the F-101A was ordered into production on 26 November 1956.

## The Landing Gear Problem

Many an Air Force pilot, and a widow or two, came to know about the Voodoo's landing gear. Bob Little, on the F-101A first flight, missed out on the variety of undercarriage glitches which marred the Voodoo's career from beginning to end. 'I had no gear problems at all other than the delayed nose gear retraction [on the first flight]. However, on a checkout flight by Brigadier General Albert G Boyd, the acceleration got away from him and he did not

retract the gear. This resulted in blowing off the landing gear doors (even the nameplates were blown off the struts). [Boyd] was at 440 knots [700 km/h] with the gear down before he was able to reduce speed. Then he put out a directive that henceforth all checkout flights in the Voodoo would be made at military power since this was more comparable to other aircraft in afterburner.' Boyd was one of the most experienced test pilots at Edwards and when Boyd got into jeopardy, it had to be asked again whether less seasoned, operational pilots would be able to cope with the F-101A.

The preceding refers to a very odd attribute of the Voodoo: beyond a certain speed, it was simply impossible to retract the nosewheel! As Colonel Jack Broughton describes it, 'The nose gear retracted forward and the system was hard-pressed to get it up into the well. If you let it accelerate the way you wanted to with all that power, before snatching the gear handle, you had a nose gear stuck down. If you pulled the nose up too sharply after takeoff, to hold the speed down, you got an immediate stall buffet as the wings blanked out the tail. It required a fine touch.' More frequently, however, landing gear failure was caused by the side brace actuator. As Robin Olds wrote the author, '[This was] the main hydraulic device for retracting and lowering the main gear. It also served as the main brace against side loads with the gear down. [It] became a source of concern as it aged and began to fail. [It] had to be remanufactured and changed throughout the aircraft fleet.' In fact, even when the Voodoo was young, the side brace actuator often caused an F-101A to plop itself down on concrete or veer off a runway. One such incident in August 1955 resulted in the number nine F-101A Voodoo (53-2426) going into the grass at St Louis' Lambert Field with one wheel collapsed. Damage, for once, was minor.

## Horizontal Control Problem

The 'link' between the pilot's artificial feel system and the Voodoo's horizontal flight control was the third of the 'terrible trio' of problems besmirching an aircraft which—it should be emphasized—was also the hottest performer of its day. The problem was the main horizontal control (slab) bell crank, hidden in the fuselage. It was the single point of contact between the bellows artificial feel system (fed back to the pilot's stick), pilot input, the trim system, the auto pilot, and the slab actuator in the vertical stabilizer. Tabs at a critical juncture in this mechanism were subject to serious metal fatigue. At one point, one of Robin Olds' personal mounts was 'in really bad shape. One tab was broken clear through, the other halfway. [It] could have gone at any time!' Had corrective measures not been taken to reinforce the strength of the tabs buried in the innards of the aircraft, Olds might have become a Voodoo casualty. To get ahead of our story, a pilot who did was Major Bud Watt, flying an F-101C Voodoo (56-0036) of

Olds' 81st Tactical Fighter Wing on approach to RAF Bentwaters, England, on 19 December 1963. Watt lost horizontal control while in the GCA pattern at Bentwaters and survived by ejecting, although he was hurt. His Voodoo was demolished.

## Flying the Voodoo

Bob Little was called upon to tell Air Force officers what they needed to know, in the March 1957 issue of

BOTTOM RIGHT
*A most* unusual *Voodoo. The 21st F-101A (54-1438) was used at Eglin AFB, Fla. in about 1955 to test a Mach 1.5 tow target for weapons firings at altitudes up to 65,000 ft (19,812 m). A stepped diameter tow cable permitted reel-out to a distance of 40,000 ft (12,192 m). This remarkable Voodoo was painted orange on its upper surfaces and natural metal on the lower side, with a black radome (USAF Armament Museum via Norman Taylor)*

*NACA operated two F-101A Voodoos, airplane 53-2434 from 22 August 1956 to 1 March 1960, and airplane 54-1442 from 18 April 1958 to 22 December 1958. Not much was done with either. The first, shown here, ended up in storage at Davis-Monthan AFB, Arizona. The second, thought never to have been photographed in NACA markings, ended up at the Sperry Corporations' aircraft graveyard (Reeder)*

the official publication *Flying Safety*. Little's remarks, reprinted here with permission, reveal much about the heavy and powerful new fighter aircraft:

'Over the past two years of development, many improvements have been incorporated into the aircraft, making it a safer and easier one for you to fly. It is not a T-33, however. I believe that the Voodoo driver needs to be a good fighter pilot as well as a good bomber pilot for the following reasons:

'You are handling more thrust per second of airplane than you have ever felt before, so it is especially important that you stay ahead of the aircraft and be prepared for the very rapid acceleration and high rates of climb possible.

'The fighter has a very high wing loading (110 pounds per square foot at normal takeoff gross weight) which means that for certain conditions, particularly high gross weight takeoffs and landings, you must handle this airplane like a highly wing-loaded bomber aircraft.

'In other words, you have a tremendous amount of thrust available and plenty of control but you can't expect to horse this airplane around with wild abandon at low airspeeds.

'Once you have the engines running and have completed your pre-taxi checklist you are ready to go. It takes a little power to start rolling. However, the thrust in idle is enough to keep you going. Use the nosewheel steering for taxying rather than differential braking. You can double the tyre life with care in taxying by using slow speeds especially when making sharp turns. The 101's power brakes have excellent feel but when coming to a full stop during taxi some brake-strut chatter may be encountered. Anticipate turns and full stops and it won't bother you.

## Takeoff

'Once you are lined up on the runway for takeoff, check each engine separately—leaving the other in idle. The brakes will hold with both engines in military [power]. However, you will probably rotate the tyres on the wheels which isn't condusive to safety. After you have checked your engines and are ready to go, advance both throttles to approximately 85 per cent rpm, depress the nosewheel steering button, release the brakes and continue to roll. Because of the ram air-bellows type artificial feel system, you will find very light stick forces on the ground. As you pick up airspeed on takeoff, these forces increase; however, during takeoff and landing they are lighter than other types of feel systems to which you might be accustomed. Therefore, during takeoff and landing don't rely on stick forces but use airspeed as a basis for proper aircraft control.

'On your initial checkout a military power takeoff is advisable since the acceleration with afterburners is terrific and may take you by surprise. Even with military power, you will have better takeoff performance than most other fighters using maximum power. Use the nosewheel steering for directional

The eleventh F-101A Voodoo (53-2428) at St Louis in August 1955. This developmental machine carries 350 US gal (291 Imp gal) under-fuselage tanks which became standard. 'Buzz number' (FB-428), used by US Air Force until 1964, can be faintly seen on underside of aircraft. Pilot's external ladder was a cumbersome, heavy device (MDC)

*Their days as strategic fighters done, these F-101C Voodoos (54-1486 and 56-0002) have reached the Kentucky Air National Guard at Standiford Airport, Louisville, Kentucky in 1965. They will train pilots of the RF-101B, RF-101C and RF-101H reconnaissance aircraft*
(via Charles W Arrington)

TOP LEFT
*Natural metal finish and a green, rather than black, anti-glare shield mark this as an early view of RF-101C Voodoo 56-0210 of the 66th Tactical Reconnaissance Wing*
(via Robert F Dorr)

LEFT
*War. Alone in a vast blue sky over Southeast Asia, an RF-101C Voodoo of the 20th Tactical Reconnaissance Squadron, the 'Green Pythons', heads towards a target near Hanoi*
(Ray Carlson)

ABOVE
*Colonel Bill Schick was commander of the 460th Tactical Reconnaissance Wing, which pitted its Voodoos against North Vietnam's formidable defences. Standing in front of an early ECM pod, he wears a Voodoo 'One-O-Wonder' shoulder patch*
(Stirling)

RIGHT
*Over North Vietnam in his single-seat RF-101C Voodoo of the 'Green Pythons,' Lt Col John Bull Stirling snapped this self-portrait of the reconnaissance pilot in combat*
(Stirling)

ABOVE
*RF-101C Voodoo 56-0105, coded AH, of the 45th Tactical Reconnaissance Squadron, the 'Polka Dots,' back from the war zone at McClellan AFB, California on 17 October 1967*
(Lars G Soldeus)

ABOVE RIGHT
*RF-101H 56-0001, or 'Balls One,' of the Kentucky Air National Guard is now a gate guardian in Louisville. Formerly, it was an F-101C strategic fighter and was flown by Colonel Robin Olds when he commanded the 81st Tactical Fighter Wing at RAF Bentwaters, England*
(Charles W Arrington)

RIGHT
*The F-101B Voodoo guarded North American skies in its interceptor role for many years. 58-0338, accompanied by a wingman, belongs to the 18th Fighter-Interceptor Squadron*
(Marty J Isham)

*EF-101B 101067, used for ECM exercises in Canadian
service, is probably the very last operational Voodoo. The
airplane's all-black paint finish is interrupted by a
temporary, natural-metal nose section, the result of a
landing gear collapse*
(Robbie Shaw)

control until the rudder becomes effective at approximately 70 knots [110 km/h] IAS [indicated air speed]. Use the brakes only if the steering malfunctions. The same old fundamentals you've been using still apply. If you ease the nose gear off at 150 knots [225 km/h] and relax stick back pressure, to hold your attitude, the airplane will fly itself off as speed increases to approximately 165 knots [240 km/h] IAS. The gear must be retracted immediately in order to avoid exceeding the gear placard of 250 knots [345 km/h] IAS. With some airplanes you know that a steep attitude will get you on the back side of the power curve and you'll never get off the runway. In this airplane, rapidly rotating into a steep attitude can get you into just as much trouble. Sure, you can horse this airplane off the ground at airspeeds lower than recommended but even with that power you can get in a bind. Why not play it cool and stay out of any difficulty?

'You will find the acceleration of the F-101 after

*The three principal missions of the Voodoo are illustrated in this August 1957 formation over St Louis. F-101A (54-1471), in foreground, is a strategic fighter with an atomic mission. RF-101A (54-1501), at right, is a photo-reconnaissance craft. F-101B (56-233), leading the pack, is an all-weather interceptor*
(MDC)

takeoff very rapid. When maximum power is used you will reach best climb speed in a minute or less (depending on temperature) after brake release. In order to maintain this climb speed the nose must be rotated steeply unless a supersonic climb is desired. You'll find it easier to maintain climb speed at maximum power with the Machmeter, and attitude with the artificial horizon. Using military power, the rate of climb is naturally lower, and the attitude is not as steep, presenting improved visibility over the nose.

'Altitudes well above the combat ceiling may be attained by employing what is known as the zoom climb. This capability holds real promise as a new tactical intercept technique for use in attacks at extremely high altitudes. It makes use of the high kinetic energy that can be developed by the Voodoo in supersonic level flight.

## Level Flight

'The level flight acceleration of this big bird is impressive at all altitudes and you will like the maximum level flight speeds attainable by the aircraft. These speeds have exceeded the original contactor estimate. Flying qualities are stable and control characteristics are positive throughout the placard speed envelope of the F-101. No wing drops or transonic speed effects are encountered. You will notice a faint airframe buffet around 0.90 Mach number. However, supersonic flight is completely smooth.

'The F-101 carries 13,000 pounds [5896 kg] of internal fuel and you will like the amount of burner flying available without having to stay in the vicinity of the base. Nevertheless, you should follow the fuel gauging procedures set forth in the Dash One [pilot's handbook] to assure that the proper sequencing is obtained and that the master fuel tank does not get too low. Extensive use of the afterburner will run you just as short as in any other airplane.

## Manoeuvring

'The Voodoo, being a true supersonic airplane, is not designed to have high manoeuvring capabilities at subsonic speeds. You will find, however, that the manoeuvring capabilities at supersonic speeds are excellent and that you will be able to maintain both Mach number and altitude during supersonic manoeuvres in a far better fashion than in any other airplane you have ever flown.

'The manoeuvrability of all fighters you've been flying was restricted by structural strength and the F-101 is no different. Again, follow your handbook placards.' Pilot Little goes into considerable detail about the pitch-up phenomenon and the workings of the Voodoo's pitch inhibitor. The narrative goes on to explain that if pitch-up instructions are ignored, the F-101A Voodoo will go into a spin from which 10,000 to 15,000 ft (3048 to 4572 m) of altitude can be lost very quickly. Then, the Voodoo's powerplant is discussed.

## Engine Operations

'The design of the F-101 is such that normal operation of all systems is available with either engine shut down. The J57 has proven to be a good, rugged engine and with two of them you can't miss unless you run out of gas. (Deadstick landings, by the way, are not on the approved list of manoeuvres for the F-101!) Engine airstarts are excellent and you will be impressed with the single engine performance of the bird. We have never encountered an engine flameout. You will find it comforting to be able to shut down an engine with no sweat if a malfunction is suspected.'

Bob Little then warns of compressor stalls and goes on to discuss the importance of playing by the book when landing the heaviest fighter in Air Force inventory. 'For an average landing with 3000 pounds [1360 kg] of fuel remaining, you should set up a smooth pattern from the base leg to flare out at 170 knots [210 km/h]. I maintain a rate of descent of about 1,000 feet [304 m] per minute using 82 per cent rpm with both engines.

'You should fly the airplane onto the runway and never try to float in that last quarter of a mile with the throttle at idle. The deceleration of the Voodoo—once you chop power and begin to flare out—will surprise you. It is on the order of five knots per second. Don't get caught in this position 50 feet in the air and a quarter mile short of the runway or you won't make it . . .'

There is more. Early F 101A Voodoos were showing unprecedented speed, endurance and staying power. Even when a couple more of them were splattered across the Mojave Desert, men came to love this airplane for its brute power and potential for winning wars. MSGT Norman Stutts: 'Daily exposure to the Voodoo for $3\frac{1}{2}$ years did not keep me from pausing to appreciate the airplane when its brakes were released, the afterburners were lit, and the F-101 sought its element.' Robin Olds: 'She could be as perverse as any female.'

There were still more perversities. The four M39 20-mm cannons mounted in the F-101A had initially been designed so that gun gas, being vented from the weapons, went into the air intake ducts and caused compressor stalls. The problem of designing a tyre which would hold up the very heavy Voodoo while still being thin enough to fit inside its thin wing was not solved until well into the the production run, when the F-101A was also redesigned to vent its gun gasses upwards. The F-101A was scheduled for delivery to SAC's 27th Strategic Fighter Wing (SFW) under Colonel Richard N Ellis in June 1956, but with Phase IV tests still under way, these and other difficulties continued to cause delays.

McDonnell had proposed building and testing the first 33 F-101As as 6.33G airplanes, then modifying the next 30 airplanes to bring them up to the 7.33G strength requirements that had been imposed by GOR 101. Under the Cook-Craigie plan, also used for the Convair F-102, an initial production run of the basic aircraft was to be kept to the minimum needed for comprehensive testing. While the test birds were being assembled, preparations would be made for full-scale production of a version that would incorporate the changes judged necessary because of the test programme. By September 1955, the Air

*An F-101A near the end of its tenure as a fighter. This Voodoo (54-1475) had returned from England to Shaw AFB, South Carolina, when photographed on 31 March 1966. This airplane was later converted to RF-101G standard and operated by the 165th TRS, Kentucky Air National Guard, at Louisville* (Norman Taylor)

Force had learned from McDonnell that F-101A production had proceeded much faster than the test programme so that the two were out of phase. It would be impossible to get a 7.33G Voodoo from the production line earlier than the 116th airframe. In June 1956, the Air Force made a decision to accept the 6.33G airplanes knowing that they could not be rebuilt for higher G stresses and would not be able to engage in aerial manoeuvres at a gross weight beyond 37,000 lb (16,782 kg). Three months later, it was

decided that the 7.33G airframes would receive the new designation F-101C.

## Homeless Waif

Eleven years after work began on a long-range penetration fighter for the Air Force, not a single F-101A Voodoo was yet in service. In spite of its unique problems, the Voodoo had proven itself again and again. It had the power, range and air-refuelling capability to fly and fight deep in the Soviet Union; its ordnance capacity was enormous; it also had the makings of an ideal reconnaissance platform and long-range interceptor. Its original purpose, to escort SAC bombers, was lost along the way, however. By 1957, the Strategic Air Command was undergoing changes in doctrine which would eventually take SAC out of the fighter business altogether.

Ironically, once it was no longer needed by SAC, the F-101A found a mission which wasn't assigned to SAC but sounded like it should have been. The F-101A Voodoo and its higher-stressed F-101C partner were to carry a centreline 'special weapon' in the nuclear strike role.

On 1 July 1957, two months after the first deliveries of the F-101A commenced far behind schedule, the 27th Strategic Fighter Wing at Bergstrom AFB, Texas, was transferred to Tactical Air Command and became the 27th Fighter-Bomber Wing (FBW). Command passed from Colonel Ellis to Colonel Charles M Walton, Jr. Converting from the F-84F Thunderstreak to the F-101A (and C) Voodoo, the wing took McDonnell's 'plane without a mission' and gave it a job—nuclear strike.

In Operation Fire Wall on 12 December 1957, Major Adrian Drew, flying an F-101A (53-2426) took the world air speed record from Great Britain by setting the mark at 1,207.6 mph (1943.43 km/h) over the 10.1-mile (16.25-km) course at Edwards. Air speed records arouse little public interest today, but in the fifties they made headlines. US JET SHATTERS RECORD, said the Chicago *Daily News*. AIR FORCE FIGHTER-BOMBER SHATTERS SPEED RECORD OF WORLD, said the Mobile *Register*. Major Drew flew to Los Angeles International Airport immediately after his achievement where he was greeted on the flight line by General Chester E McCarty, commander 18th Air Force, who presented him with a DFC.

## Eniwetok Atoll

An F-101A was assigned to Project Redwing on Bikini and Eniwetok Atolls in the Pacific. The Voodoo lived in a world where hydrogen bombs were exploded in the atmosphere and the US and Soviet Union seemed bent on constantly increasing the megatonnage of the weapons they set off. The object of Redwing was to define the limits of bomb effects the F-101A could stand and also to test its delivery

TOP LEFT
*Final configuration for an F-101A. A-model Voodoos like this one (54-1462) were converted to RF-101G standard for Air National Guard reconnaissance duties. This one had been called to active duty and was heading west towards Korea's* Pueblo *crisis when the incomparable camera of Norman Taylor caught it at Elmendorf AFB, Alaska, on 21 August 1968*
(Norman Taylor)

*The end of the road. Some single-seat Voodoo fighters never served operationally. Given a J prefix to signify minor changes in its role as a developmental aircraft, JF-101A (53-2445) basks in the sun at the Military Storage and Disposition Center (MASDC) in Arizona on 20 April 1961, destined to fly no more*
(Douglas D Olson)

capabilities. The Voodoo never actually dropped The Bomb, but the tests proved that it could. Major John Apple was the pilot, Captain Melvin Lewin led the Air Force activity, and MAC's people were led by E F Peters. After a mishap on its westward ferry trip which required rapid repairs at Wright Field, the F-101A flew on to Eniwetok to participate in several thermonuclear detonations.

During Major Apple's repeated flights through mushroom clouds, his biggest problem was inside the canopy. This was the burning and the smoke produced by black surfaces over the instrument panel, on the canopy sill, and on the antenna lead-ins on the rear deck. The F-101A was equipped with a radiation hood which was modified at the site to exclude as much light as possible. In the smaller shots, the pilots felt that the hood—two layers of white duck, one with an aluminum painted surface on the common side—would be adequate eye protection. But Apple was also equipped at all times with dark glasses similar to welder's goggles.

The airplane was instrumented for gust, thermal and nuclear effects from the bombs. Technical studies were made to enable positioning of the airplane and definition of the speed and altitude to result in safe impignment of these effects. A technical team was trained to maintain the instrumentation and to accomplish rapid changeovers called for in Redwing where the Voodoo people worked at the convenience of the bomb shooters and had to adapt to the latter's schedules. E F Peters noted that the superior maintainability of the F-101A was a solid asset which resulted in the airplane being on-line for all but one test. This test was missed because a certain ring seal for the cockpit was not foreseen as a necessary spare and its delivery was delayed by the crash of a supply airplane.

With the size and weight of atomic bombs being reduced and the F-101A (and F-101C) assigned to carry the weapons—a job also to be given to some of the reconnaissance variants of the Voodoo—Project Redwing confirmed that the F-101A could operate in a nuclear environment and not be harmed by the blast. The test airplane went into locations where the bomb ripped, tore and heated it and flew home blackened and rippled. When an H-bomb was airdropped by a B-52 Stratofortress, Major Apple took the F-101A through the mushroom cloud at supersonic speed—the first time that this had been done.

The 'acceptance' airframe which made the Voodoo operational was the 41st F-101A built. Of 77 F-101As accepted, 50 reached combat forces, the remainder being 'preproduction' machines used for tests and a variety of projects. Eventually, the F-101A and F-101C were virtually indistinguisable when they served together. For the A model, some handy math expert had concluded that the airplane had an average maintenance cost of $362.00 per flying hour and that the flyaway cost per production aircraft was $2,906,373 for the airframe, $2,364,143 more for engines (installed), $429,016 for electronics, $25,249 for ordnance and $72,665 for armament. In 1956, the year which lay in the centre of the F-101A Voodoo delivery schedule, a Chevrolet four-door sedan could be purchased for $1,800 and a four-bedroom family bungalow sold for $25,000. McDonnell's first production airplane for the Air Force was expensive, as things went. But no price was too high if the Air Force was to be properly equipped. And on the far side of the Atlantic the Russians were being more strident than ever.

It was time for the Voodoo to move to Europe.

# Chapter 4
# The Heyday of the Bentwaters Bombers
## Perfecting the F-101C in Peacetime

The 81st Tactical Fighter Wing at RAF Bentwaters/Woodbridge, England, was the *only* outfit ever to fly the Voodoo fighter in foreign skies. 'It had to be the best peacetime fighter wing the Air Force has ever seen,' says Lt Col Robert A Hanson, who was there.

First deliveries of the F-101C Voodoo were made to Bergstrom in September 1957 and, except for their structural tolerance to G forces, the A and C models of the fighter were essentially interchangeable. In May 1957, delivery of the 47th and last F-101C, following after 77 airframes in the F-101A series, put the Voodoo fighter out of production before it ever saw Europe. Once, *three* wings of Voodoo fighters had been planned. Fighters still on the production line would be converted to the reconnaissance role instead. In that sense, a mighty warplane with superb performance seemed still, to be searching for a role and a home.

## The Pentagon and the F-101A/C

The 'orphan' Voodoo's first major move, as noted, was from SAC to TAC. General Curtis E LeMay, the tough-as-nails SAC chief, had given up his strategic fighter wings rather than be forced by budget cuts to inactivate his B-58 Hustler force. Having gotten rid of an entire fleet of fighters which he'd never liked anyway (F-84Fs, plus the Bergstrom F-101A/Cs), LeMay then moved to the Pentagon as vice chief of staff to continue the dominance of bomber men in the Air Force. This left no *raison d'etre* for the 27th TFW at Bergstrom, which became a prime target for the budget-cutter's axe. Fighter-Bomber Wings (FBW) were later redesignated Tactical Fighter Wings (TFW) on 7 July 1958 and the latter term is used henceforth for simplicity. The solution to the budget problem was to declare that the F-101A/C was 'all-weather,' which nobody had ever claimed before, and

to shift the upstart orphan across an ocean. A proposal was made to retire the F-84Fs at Bentwaters in Great Britain and to retain one wing of F-101A/Cs which would move from Bergstrom to Bentwaters. Additional Voodoos not yet flying would become photo-reconnaissance machines. The men and airplanes of the 27th TFW at Bergstrom would move to RAF Bentwaters/Woodbridge to upgrade the 81st TFW.

The only problem was, the senior Air Force officer in Europe didn't *want* one unique wing of aircraft to complicate his logistics and operational problems. In 1957–58, the Commander of United States Air Forces in Europe (USAFE) was General Frank F Everest, who should not be confused with Lt Col (later Brig Gen) Frank K (Pete) Everest, test pilot of the XF-88 and F-101A. A series of 'Dear Curt' and 'Dear Frank' informal cables began to fly back and forth between LeMay in the Pentagon and Everest in Wiesbaden—LeMay seemingly trying to get Everest to accept an airplane he hadn't wanted himself, Everest resisting the Voodoo. The 'Dear Frank' portion of the exchange was drafted not by the bomber general but by an eloquent lieutenant colonel who had begun flying the Voodoo at Edwards, John Bull Stirling.

From the start, Stirling seems to have been immensely fond of the airframe he would later take into North Vietnam, in a war planned by bomber generals but carried out by fighter pilots. Stirling had gone to Edwards where Major Adrian Drew checked him out in the F-101A, flying the Voodoo on 7 December 1955 as the 43rd Air Force officer to solo the type. He recalls that, 'the first takeoff was spectacular, with the acceleration breathtaking.' The Voodoo was not always unforgiving to John Bull Stirling, however:

'One afternoon I was preparing for a flight at Eglin AFB [in the Florida panhandle where Air Proving

*Before leaving Bergstrom AFB, Texas, for England, F-101A/C Voodoo fighters wore colourful tail markings, as in this example of the 524th TFS, 27th TFW seen in July 1957. 524th TFS had blue tail colours whilst companion 522nd TFS has red, 523rd yellow, and 481st green. 20 mm cannon ports are covered as this Voodoo taxies in trailing brake chute (MDC)*

TOP RIGHT
*The C model Voodoo in England. F-101C (56-0018) of the 81st TFW at RAF Bentwaters on 11 May 1963 (*Norman Taylor collection*)*

RIGHT
*The 81st TFW operated both F-101A and F-101C aircraft in England. F-101A Voodoo (54-1470) at RAF Bentwaters in October 1964 (*S Peltz via Norman Taylor*)*

Ground Command carried out ordnance tests] and the maintenance crew asked me to make a high-speed fly-by down the flight line. The control tower cleared me in from Crestview north of Eglin. I recall seeing over 700 knots [1150 km/h] crossing the airfield out of a dive and experiencing hard jolts from the choppy air at 500 feet [152 m] above the ground. I activated the afterburners and started a 5G pullup reaching a nose-up angle of maybe 50 degrees when the seat which was in the full-up position suddenly became unlatched as though someone had pulled a trigger. I felt that my spine had been struck with a sledgehammer. I was violently doubled over, knocking the wind out of me. My instant perception was that the airplane had exploded. My hand on the control stick induced a series of violent rocking motions in the longitudinal axis that were most alarming to the spectators. I regained my senses going over the top at nineteen thousand feet [5781 m] and rolled over to recover. For a minute I was almost afraid to move my body for fear of injury. When the seat bottomed, the pain was sharp and severe.' Stirling has never had back problems since, however, and the Voodoo was provided with an electrically adjustable seat.

Almost as comfortable with a typewriter as with a control stick, Stirling drew the hapless task of drafting the cable which would say that LeMay supported the Voodoo (which he didn't) and make Everest want to accept the aircraft (which *he* didn't). In later years, Stirling would be stalked by flak, missiles and MiGs, but dealing face-to-face with cigar-chewing General LeMay was the ultimate test of courage. Legend holds that early in his SAC days, a foolhardy officer tried to persuade LeMay not to smoke his cigar while standing dangerously close to a fuel-filled KC-97 tanker. Forgetting that the SAC band painted around the flying gas station might as well have meant that LeMay owned it, the officer had warned that the cigar might cause the tanker to blow up. 'Blow *up*?' retorted LeMay. 'It wouldn't *dare*!'

While Stirling hunkered down in his Pentagon office to compose the latest 'Dear Frank'—with considerable discomfort—the Voodoo made at least a temporary visit to Europe.

## CASF Deployment

In the late 1950s, Tactical Air Command (temporary owner of the orphan) was married to the Composite Air Strike Force (CASF) concept. In a crisis, which might erupt anywhere from Formosa to Berlin, the CASF concept required plans for swift reaction, deployment of men and machines with maximum speed, and an immediate adjustment to operations at a distant overseas location. During the July 1958 Lebanon crisis, while F-100 Super Sabres were rushed from stateside bases to Adana, Turkey, and other locations, the Voodoo was taken across an ocean.

At the 27th TFW at Bergstrom, one of the squadron commanders was Major John J ('JJ') Burns, a future wearer of major general's stars who was to remain a fond advocate of the Voodoo for life. Burns commanded the wing's 522nd TFS. On 28 July 1958, Burns led four F-101Cs from Andrews AFB, Maryland to Bierset AB, Belgium, not as a direct part of the buildup which accompanied the landing of Marines in Lebanon but, instead, to impress NATO luminaries at an air show.

Three times, Burns' F-101Cs took on fuel from newly-developed KC-135A Stratotankers, creating an apparition which never looked right to the eye: the tanker, churning along in its typical slightly nose-down attitude while the Voodoo hung on to the boom as if for dear life, at the contrastingly very high angle of attack the fighter was famous for. Weather conditions were near-treacherous throughout much of the 3,455 nautical mile (6100 km) flight which was completed in an unprecedented six hours, eleven minutes. While policymakers stirred up a second crisis at Formosa to go along with the one in Lebanon, warriors like Burns showed a curious crowd that the F-101C was not merely big but mean. Burns did some fancy flying, in the days before stodgy rules about maintaining distance from crowds. On one occasion, he showed that the F-101C had better takeoff acceleration than the vaunted F-104 Starfighter. The detachment from Burns' squadron took the F-101C on tour to Soesterburg AB, Holland, RAF Bentwaters (future home of the 81st TFW) and Nouasseur AB, Morocco, before returning stateside. The stage was set for the 81st TFW to convert to the Voodoo. At least, if Frank Everest could be persuaded.

## The Pentagon and the F-101A/C (II)

In the Pentagon, Colonel Chesley Peterson instructed the typewriter-wielding Lt Col John Bull Stirling to draft a not-too-thinly disguised message reflecting loss of patience and telling General Everest and his USAFE staff to stop resisting the Voodoo.

TOP RIGHT
*Typical of the Voodoo pilot of the 1960s, when the 81st TFW was the only wing in the US Air Force operating the type, Capt Robert Hanson climbs aboard his F-101A (54-1482) in about 1961*
*(Hanson)*

RIGHT
*The patchwork countryside of East Anglia had seen its share of American warplanes already, but none was more impressive than the single-seat fighter version of the 'One Oh Wonder.' F-101C Voodoo (56-0012) of the Bentwaters-based 81st TFW flies over England in about 1964. Not readily visible in background are two more F-101A/C aircraft, accompanied by a pair of F-100 Super Sabres*
*(courtesy Robin Olds)*

Since the 'Dear Frank' ultimatum had to be signed by LeMay, it seemed a 'no win' situation.

On a Sunday morning, Stirling went to the Pentagon, met a general, and accompanied him to General LeMay's office. He'd brought his 'Dear Frank' message which had been coordinated, a flip-chart briefing which explained the message, and an oversized but handsome desk model of the F-101C taken from a large display model case in the hallway outside the vice chief of staff's office. Stirling boldly placed the model on General LeMay's desk and proceeded to praise the long range and high performance of the aircraft. The general, wearing civilian clothes for once but with the inevitable cigar in his mouth, stared at the model 'as though I had put something on his desk which smelled badly. Curtis E LeMay had little time for fighter type aircraft.'

Stirling pressed on with his briefing. He seemed to have LeMay's attention as well as a half dozen senior staff people who sat around the general listening. He flipped over a new chart and started down a list of Voodoo strong points, including—now that a stroke of the pen had made it an all-weather craft—'the F-101's ability to penetrate deeply into the Soviet heartland under all-weather conditions.' At this point, General LeMay took the cigar from his mouth and with a firm voice announced, 'That's a bunch of shit!' Stirling looked around and saw everybody grinning at him but contributing nothing. He pressed on and, moments later, to his astonishment, LeMay relented. 'Let me see that message.' He read it and without comment signed it. The F-101s were going into Bentwaters, period. Having survived an ordeal greater than what lay ahead in the Barrel, Stirling gathered up his message, his flip chart briefing and the Voodoo model and 'got the hell out of there.'

## Formosa Fighter

While still operating at Bergstrom in late 1958, the Voodoo fighter deployed to Formosa during a time of heightened tension. (Americans did not call the island Taiwan at that time). An artillery duel was raging over the postage-stamp islands of Quemoy and Matsu and the author, in the Air Force at the time, recalls being issued a dosimeter in anticipation of atomic war. F-86F Sabres of the Chinese Nationalist Air Force made MiG-17 kills in the first use of a new weapon, the AAM-N-7 (later redesignated AIM-9) Sidewinder heat-seeking missile. The Sidewinder was to become one of the most numerous and successful aerial weapons of the twentieth century and the ubiquitous Major John J Burns, who made it to Formosa too, felt the missile had potential for the Voodoo. Because of its wide turning radius, the F-101A/C might be vulnerable to interception by MiGs with missiles of their own unless it, too, was so armed.

Major Burns obtained an AAM-N-7 Sidewinder missile and rigged an F-101C Voodoo (56-0027) for a test-firing on 25 November 1958. This is thought to

be the only time the fighter Voodoo ever fired an air-to-air missile. The test seems to have been successful, but Burns' 522nd TFS returned from Formosa to Bergstrom before further tests could be taken. When the men and machines later shifted to Europe, 'low and fast' strike tactics developed for a European conflict rendered an air-to-air missile unnecessary.

It was a placid setting in the flatland and greenery of East Anglia's twin airbases of RAF Bentwaters and RAF Woodbridge where the 81st TFW flew F-101A/C Voodoos from December 1958 to January 1966. The wing operated Voodoos with its three squadrons, the 78th TFS (Bushmasters), 91st TFS (Blue Streaks) and 92nd TFS (Avengers). Many of the young warriors who flew the single-seat strategic Voodoo with the wing are now wearing stars, like General Robert D Russ, today's chief of Tactical Air Command, who was a lieutenant from May 1957 to May 1960 when he transitioned from F-84F Thunderstreak to F-101A Voodoo. Russ will also be encountered in the later story of the interceptor variant of the Voodoo.

81st TFW commander Colonel Henry L Crouch, Jr established a diligent programme to prepare pilots and maintenance people for the new machine. As one pilot says, 'The 81st TFW birds were very, very enjoyable to fly, yet the old Voodoo demanded a measure of respect. She'd go like hell, had long legs, a modified air-to-air radar dedicated to air-to-ground, three 20-mm cannons [the fourth taken out to make space for a transponder], two droptank hardpoints, and a centreline store point.' To emphasize again the Voodoo's main purpose, the store point was for a tactical atomic bomb which was the only thing the Voodoo could carry with any practical effect.

## Soviet Response

Was it a cost-efficient move to operate just one wing (54 airframes) of F-101A/C Voodoos in the very crowded NATO readiness environment, where numbers *were* important and commonality of parts and supplies was always a problem? It might be remembered that in 1957–58, the US Air Force in Europe, like the Royal Air Force, was at the peak of its strength, operating no fewer than eight fighter wings. Did it make sense to insert just one wing of the one-of-a-kind Voodoo when the cost of maintaining each airframe must have been several times the cost of, say, an F-100? Apparently the Russians thought so.

An article in the Soviet air force's official journal, *Herald of the Red Air Fleet*, written by a Russian officer unaware of the teething pains of the Voodoo, slurred the Americans for bringing 'a new type of atomic bomber' to England. (In both languages, the word 'atomic' was as widely used then as 'nuclear' is today). In a surprising admission, it was noted that the F-101A/C Voodoo was an exceptionally fast warplane with respectable range and load-carrying

*F-101C Voodoos (56-0018, at left, and 56-0026) of the
81st TFW in flight over the British coast near Oxford,
Suffolk, southeast of RAF Woodbridge. Markings indicate
that photo was taken after 1962, when the 81st TFW went
to the '66-01 maintenance scheme' and the aircraft of all
squadrons were painted the same. Just barely visible
beneath 56-0018 is the tail hook just aft of the
afterburners—a retrofit*
(Hanson)

capability. In the brinkmanship which prevailed in
those days before arms talks, it was suggested that
Moscow would have to make 'appropriate response'
to the Voodoo. It cannot be proven, but the
F-101A/C may have led to an increase in Soviet
expenditure on air defence systems, including the
SA-2 *Guideline* surface-to-air missile (SAM) which
would alter combat tactics forever in two years' time.

'The world's most powerful operational fighters,'
as one journal called them, began to arrive with the
81st TFW in December 1958 when Major Walter
Eichelberger repeated Burns' trans-Atlantic journey
of six months earlier. Eichelberger took seven
F-101A/Cs from Bergstrom to Bentwaters, covering
5,199 miles (8318 km) in eleven hours, one minute
with two KC-135A refuellings. Among those who
accompanied him were record-holder Major Adrian
Drew and Major Brian J Lincoln, the latter
nicknamed 'Cadillac Jack'—both destined to be

squadron commanders in the 81st TFW.

The close-knit team of fighter pilots at Bergstrom
who'd transitioned from F-84F to F-101A/C (and
from SAC to TAC) was now dismantled. The men
and machines of the sun-drenched Texas setting
moved to the rain and murk of East Anglia. For those
already at Bentwaters and Woodbridge, there was a
brief exposure to the sun when men from England
and airframes from Bergstrom were temporarily
brought together for a few weeks of training at
George AFB in southern California. These pilots
who would make up the 81st TFW, including the
veterans who came from Bergstrom, had in common
with the pilots of reconnaissance Voodoos of the same
period the accidental fortune of being the most
experienced fighter jocks in the Air Force. At times,
they needed to be.

In October 1960, Captain Jack E Shephard of the
91 TFS/81 TFW was making a GCA letdown over
the North Sea when, after lowering his gear, his
F-101C Voodoo's throttles became stuck. Shephard
began to sink. The Voodoo exhibits the aerodynamic
qualities of an anvil under certain conditions and a
markedly concerned Shephard found himself rapidly
losing altitude whilst unable to budge his throttles.
Normal backup methods to 'un-stick' the power
control refused to work. The Voodoo kept plummet-
ing downward. Shephard was in danger of crossing

the 900-ft (274-m) altitude mark, below which the Voodoo's ejection seat was not considered safe. Shepard took the unusual step of unstrapping himself (thus giving up the alternative of ejecting) and raising his leg in order to push hard on the throttles with his foot. The extra strength provided a rudimentary solution to the problem and, using his foot on the throttles and releasing his para-brake early on approach, Shephard recovered safely at Bentwaters.

## Low-Level Mission

Even to these seasoned veterans, the low-level nuclear strike mission—destination, Russia—was a challenge. From 1 May 1960 when a SAM missile downed Francis Gary Powers' U-2 spy plane near the Soviet industrial city of Sverdlovsk, it was never again possible to do business at high altitudes where bombers and fighter-bombers had, until then, roamed with ease. Even prior to his move from Texas to East Anglia to command a squadron of the 81st TFW (he had the 92nd TFS), Major Burns spearheaded the development of an all-weather, low-level nuclear delivery using the Voodoo's gun-ranging radar which had a ground mapping mode. The airplane's Low Altitude Bombing System (LABS) and its later Low Angle Drogued Delivery (LADD) delivery systems were highly respectable for the period, but not easy to master. It is worth remembering that the F-101A/C was only provided

with 20-mm guns and the centreline nuclear weapon. Two 450-gallon auxiliary drop tanks straddled the centreline weapon, although pilots who were interviewed years later disagreed as to whether the airplane could carry both fuel tanks and The Bomb at the same time. There were no hard points on the wings for external bomb racks, so there wasn't much in the way of a non-nuclear mission that the airplane could perform—although Burns drilled his men relentlessly in 20-mm strafing tactics.

Without sophisticated terrain-avoidance or inertial navigation systems in these early days of the nuclear strike mission, the men of the 81st TFW were expected to take their Voodoos solo at 50 ft (17 m) of altitude, making use of the LABS/LADD maze of gyros, timers and computers which plugged known factors into onboard computers to determine when a bomb should be released and to make the automatic release.

Except for a few tentative efforts during the Korean conflict, air-to-air refuelling had never been used during an actual combat mission. It was not yet part of the 'mind set' to expect air refuelling to be there when needed. Yet the men at Bentwaters and Woodbridge planned straight-line runs into East Germany, Poland and the Soviet Union, to targets as distant as 2,000 miles (3200 km), knowing that available tanker assets might be needed by SAC bombers and that Voodoo pilots, having lower priority, might not get the fill-up of gas needed for a

*F-101A Voodoos (54-1452) of the 81st TFW at RAF Bentwaters near the end of the tenure of this aircraft type in July 1965. The composite (wing, rather than squadron) markings on this Voodoo's tail were adopted in 1962 along with centralized wing maintenance. Colours from top to bottom are blue, yellow and red*
(via Clyde Gerdes)

BELOW
*F-101C Voodoo of the 81st TFW at RAF Bentwaters, England, arrives at Wheelus AB, Libya, during a 1964 deployment for weapons practice. Note the dummy nuclear store mounted under the fuselage*
(courtesy Robin Olds)

round trip. Certainly, the men did not consider themselves candidates for suicide missions, but when they looked at intelligence reports on Soviet troop concentrations in the East (satellite photos being a thing of the future), they must have wondered what would happen to them and their Voodoos after contributing to an atomic Armageddon.

A bit of a newcomer to the highly-seasoned Bergstrom Mob bound for Bentwaters was 1st Lt Duane E (Whitey) Boye, a Kansas boy who started out with another of the three squadrons under the 27th TFW, this being the 524th TFS commanded by Major James Doolittle, Jr. Boye was at the time the most junior officer and the first of first-lieutenant rank, to fly the Voodoo. Boye ferried an aircraft from Bergstrom to George where the East Anglia folks were being trained. His life then departed the single-seat Voodoo scene, briefly. The lieutenants drew cards to see who'd get the much-wanted posting to join the 81st TFW at Bentwaters. Boye ended up, instead, at Hamilton AFB, California flying two-seat F-101B Voodoos for a year. This was ADC (Air Defense Command), a different life, and it wasn't for Boye. He wasn't surprised when his commander took him to lunch one day, talked straight talk, and arranged a transfer to Bentwaters—by now, fully converted to the Voodoo.

The three squadrons of the 81st TFW flew their Voodoos down to Wheelus AB, Libya—a friendly nation then, with King Idris in power—to practice live ordnance drops. The base near Tripoli was crowded with American warplanes from all over Europe.

To take over an 81st TFW squadron at Bentwaters (the 92nd TFS) came Lt Col Daniel (Chappie) James. James was a good, but not great, fighter pilot. He was also a superb leader, able to whip together a squadron in peacetime and to lead men into battle in war. Chappie James was a negro, the noun black having not yet entered the American language in 1962, and had flown P-51D Mustangs in World War 2 in an all-negro squadron before the armed forces were desegregated by President Truman. James later attained four-star rank. In 1962, Lt Col James demanded and got top performance from the 92nd TFS (Avengers). He took the squadron down to Wheelus frequently for realistic training. Wheelus was, as has been said, an exceedingly crowded base, handling fighter traffic from all over the USAFE command, and while pilots liked to go there, they did not like the base's fuelling area.

Lt Whitey Boye, who of course addressed as James as 'colonel' when not using a radio callsign, remembers the Wheelus fuelling area vividly. 'You had to taxi in their on your own power, and the Voodoo was a very hot airplane with both engines turning, so you always had the fear of flying.' On a day when many aircraft of various types were circling the field and using the same radio frequency, Boye was on the ground following Chappie James into the fuel pits when a sudden fire erupted under James' Voodoo. The abrupt flicker of flames was enough to instill sudden terror. Afraid that half the airbase would go up in flames, including himself, Boye was momentarily at a total loss to remember James' radio callsign. 'You're on fire!' he shouted. 'Get out of that airplane, colonel!' Boye's version of the story is that no fewer than 16 colonels and lieutenant colonels were airborne in the Wheelus pattern and that, because he forgot to use a callsign, all 16 of them—James included—ejected.

The story has numerous flaws, including the fact that ejection seats were not zero-zero in those days, but it conveys the spirit and humour of the men who flew—and were ready to fight—in the single-seat Voodoo. Were they fearful of their atomic mission behind the Iron Curtain? The Cuban missile crisis affected the 81st TFW, too. Lt Col Robert A Hanson: 'I came walking into the Operations area and all the bomb commanders were gathered around the nuclear duty officer's desk. He was copying a message from Headquarters. I had on my slippers, flight suit, a cup of coffee . . . I leaned over his shoulder. I noticed on the message format that the duty officer had written a Red Delta Alpha message. We all knew that was a mistake. It should have been a White Delta Alpha, which was the term for an exercise.' It quickly turned out that it was no exercise and that the wing was really being placed on nuclear alert. Hanson continues:

'Our job was to go in and soften up their air order of battle while the SAC pukes hit their strategic targets. We sat cockpit alert all day. We were in the airplane with the power on, ready to hit the button and go. My particular target was an airfield in Poland. I had no doubt we could hit it. We had pre-strike tankers out over the North Sea but no post-strike tankers. It seemed that most of the tanker assets were reserved for the SAC pukes. We had enough fuel to get in, strike the target, and turn up into the vast Polish forest and eject. The idea was to sit there for a couple of weeks and wait until the fallout subsided, then E & E [perform escape and evasion] and make your way up to the Baltic and get picked up by a friendly submarine. It was a good story and I guess we bought it. Anyway, there we sat all day . . . and it was a 24 hour operation . . . on alert day and night . . .'

Chappie James was promoted to full colonel and left his squadron to become ADO (assistant deputy for operations) and later DO (deputy for operations) of the 81st TFW. It remained for a new wing commander to arrive so that the legendary team could be put together consisting of 'Blackman and Robin.'

## Enter Robin Olds

Olds was, is, the greatest fighter wing commander ever to serve in the US Air Force—although, as will be seen, his superiors did not view it that way during the 81st TFW period. He is the only officer of whom the author can say that no one who ever served with him, from his enlisted armourers to his star-studded bosses, ever uttered the first criticism—except, as will be seen, when he tried to make the Voodoo aerobatic. In 1963, Colonel Robin Olds had been an All-America tackle on the West Point football team and a fighter ace in World War 2. He'd married an actress. Ahead of him lay towering achievements in North Vietnamese skies but in 1963 Colonel Robin Olds was assigned to take command of the 81st TFW. He would fly 307:20 hours in the F-101A/C.

Notified that he would take over the wing in August 1963, Olds arranged in July for a checkout in the F-101 Voodoo at Tyndall AFB, Florida. He spent about three weeks accumulating 15 to 20 hours in the F-101B interceptor version. He arrived at Bentwaters to find the F-101A/C far more enjoyable than the B model.

This seems the place for Robin Olds' observations, supplied for this volume, on two of the Voodoo's good points, of which, Olds adds, 'There are really too many to enumerate.

'*Stability*. Low level. Like a rock. A true pleasure to run our practice delivery routes.

'*Radar*. Air-to-air originally. Modified by a brilliant officer named J J Burns [already encountered in this narrative] for air-to-ground work. It had options for 200-mile, 100-mile, 80-mile, 40-, 20-, 10-, and 5-mile ranges. Low level radar navigation was a fascinating challenge. The pilot had to know where he was by the basic of all basics— compass, watch, ground speed, and compensate for winds. Then tour time cross-hatched course line on your map could be related to the imaged return on your radar scope. Then you could be certain that the blip 15 miles ahead, 2 degrees left, was indeed the steel mill gantry in, say, Manchester, which might be your intended practice target.'

## Mission to Scotland

To illustrate the low-level navigation essential to the Voodoo nuclear mission, Robin Olds describes a flight in the clinging wet bogs and valleys of Scotland, where American fighter-bomber pilots have tested their mettle for two generations. 'We had a high-low-high route that took us up to the east coast, past Teamborough Head (a wonderful radar check point), Tees Bay, Tynemouth, and to a turn off the Firth of Jay. There, left and start a letdown, steering for the next turn point, going down to 1,000 ft [304 m]. The point was Ordmucknish Bay, just east of Lismore Island in the Firth of Lorn. A glance at the map will show you that this point was well below the mountain tops in that part of Scotland. This was indeed a 'dicey' turn point. You *had* to be right. Then down southward at 500 ft (152 m) past Colonsay and Islay, a course correction to the left, and south-southeast for the Isle of Man, using Stranraer at the south end of Loch Ryan for an offset radar checkpoint. Our destination was a large target some miles off the east coast of Man, somewhere near Clayhead. There an observer would plot the smoke flare of our bomb release. (We used a practice device having the same ballistics as the Big Boy). Often, this entire low-level portion would be flown in cloud, completely on the gauges, including the pattern used to set up for a run-in at 540 knots at 500 ft [900 km/h at 152 m] above sea level. All of this was done by the pilot himself. He navigated, flew the bird, set up the run, and dropped the practice device. And a damned fine challenge it was!'

Actually begun at least two years earlier by Brian J Lincoln, alias Cadillac Jack, the custom of using radio callsigns based on automobile brands became not merely a word-play on Lincoln's surname but, as

When it deployed to Wheelus AB, Libya, the Voodoo-equipped 81st TFW brought everything, including a signboard. On 13 December 1960, Capt Robert Hanson stands in front of a Wheelus sign naming wing commander Col Eugene L Strickland, Maj Harry K Barco, Lt Col John J Burns and Maj Brian J Lincoln. It was 'Cadillac Jack' Lincoln who began the custom of using radio callsigns after automobiles, a practice continued by 1963 wing commander Robin Olds (courtesy Lt Col Robert Hanson))

*Colonel Robin Olds, commander of the 81st Tactical Fighter Wing at RAF Bentwaters, England, in the cockpit of his F-101C Voodoo in 1964. Colourful helmets, to go with colourful tail markings, were in vogue at this time. Note radar scope on the left side of the cockpit, close to the camera*
(courtesy Robin Olds)

well, on Olds'—OLDS flight, FORD flight, RAMBLER flight, and so on—and was later employed by Olds for his well-known MiG-killing operations in Vietnam. Olds describes another trip in the F-101A/C Voodoo:

'This time we're leaving Bentwaters on a Sunday afternoon. Our destination is Wheelus AB, down on the north coast of Africa at Tripoli, Libya. We're going down for a week, maybe two, of range work at El Outia. We have two drop tanks and some clothes and our toilet articles. There could be a few spare parts stuffed in the ammo trays for the maintenance troops at Wheelus. We're going non-stop, some 1,500 miles [2400 km].' Because of the timing of the author's interview with Olds, he pointed out that this was the same route which the French government had refused American warplanes to use when Libya itself became a target in April 1986. 'That's okay. We have the range. So off we leap, climbing out through the cloud decks, seaching our initial altitude of 28,000 ft [8524 m] heading for Dover.

'We check in with British Air Control. Cleared as filed. An ICAO call at Dover. Permission to enter French air space? Long pause. Permission granted 'de facto,' meaning normal. We're told by French control to descend to 24,000 ft [7225 m]. We reply, "Roger, descending." Instead, we go up, as planned, for fuel reasons.' The long friendship between the US and France has always been an ambivalent one, and apparently it was not uncommon for Voodoo pilots to put it to the test.

## Voodoo versus Mirage

'Soon the Mirages intercept us,' continues Olds, apparently referring to Mirage IIIC aircraft stationed at Dijon. The French pilots are aware that the Voodoo is faster than they are and that they, but not the Voodoo pilots, must worry about fuel consumption. 'We decide to give them the finger, American style. We lift our refuelling probes, exactly like a rigid middle digit, and press on. Past Lyon, we coast out near Marseille, down past Sardinia and Corsica. There's Pantellerca on the scope now and Tunis off to the right, Malta on the left. Navigation's a piece of cake and the temperature is 100°F plus. Quickly there is Libya, the city of Tripoli sticking out like the old sore thumb, even the Quay prominent as we get nearer, let down, and enter the pattern. We set up for landing on [runway] 27, break left, and hear "flaps down" for that big, beautiful runway and a welcoming beer.'

Working out with the F-101A/C Voodoo on the range at Wheelus is a Cold War exercise Olds remembers vividly. Was he one of the 16 colonels who ejected in Boye's fantasy? He won't say.

'On the range. You're going to do an "over the shoulder" [delivery of a simulated atomic bomb]. You set the figures in the computer system before climbing in. You've done your LABS check on the way to El Outia, you've coasted in at Sabratha (old Roman city) and you called the range for clearance. You take spacing and now you're headed down the run-in line. You're motoring at 540/560 knots and you're about 50 feet off the deck. There's the target, a couple of boilers welded end to end, filled with sand, painted white and upright in the middle of the target ring. You whistle over the aim point, allowing for wind, and start your pull. Wings level, 2 Gs, pointers centred. Up, up you go in a great Immelman, keeping everything centred. The practice bomb is released when you're about 120 degrees through the manoeuvre. It goes up.

'Now it's time for your escape manoeuvre.' If this were the real thing, with the bomb still headed upward, a minute might remain until a gigantic white flash that will fill the air behind the Voodoo pilot.

'You come across the top, let the nose fall through, hit afterburners, and haul ass for the horizon. Meanwhile, the bomb has topped out at about 22 thou [6677 m], turned over and started down. If all has gone well you'll get a 300-footer [within 300 ft or 100 m of the target] and that's great. The real thing doesn't have to hit that close to destroy New York City. But you've done this basically on instruments and would do so under actual conditions. In practice, you do three or four laydowns and some strafing, fiddling with the switches between each pass, hoping you do well—for the critics at the bar are vociferous and some small sums of money have been known to change hands on the outcome of your day's efforts.'

Olds organized the first and only F-101A/C Voodoo aerobatic display while in the UK. This was technically impossible and it caused him to be sacked. They still talk of it, Voodoo pilots. They talk of the aerobatic performance as one of the all-time displays of flying skill and entertainment ever witnessed. They love it, Voodoo pilots do. But the exhibition caused Olds' name to be removed from the brigadier general's list and he eventually ended up, instead, commanding the 8th TFW in Ubon with Phantoms—'which was what I wanted in the first place.'

There is no question that Colonel Robin Olds loved the Voodoo. 'She set me up well for the work to be done later in the Phantom and I served with truly outstanding people, many of whom joined me later in Thailand . . .'

With drogued (i.e., parachute-retarded) atomic weapons entering inventory, the LADD technique superseded the LABS method in about 1963. The Immelman turn described by Olds as the Voodoo pilot's standard escape—putting the nuclear airburst behind him as quickly as possible—was unusual for an aircraft which had never accommodated itself well to gravity stresses (or aerobatics!) Immelman turns were not performed at all in later Voodoos but were routinely carried out even on instruments, in bad weather and at night, in the F-101A/C. An alternate method of bomb delivery, using the F-101A/C model's Mergenthaler Linotype M-1 Toss Bombing System (TBS-1) enabled the pilot to deliver his 'special weapon'—an unfortunate euphemism—by lining up the target on the crosshairs of his K-19 gunsight and pushing a button which computed an automatic release. Pilots did not find that the TBS-1 system offered any improvement over the Immelman-toss method and it was not employed much in the European setting.

Renowned for its stability as a flying machine, the F-101A/C Voodoo was a better gun platform than is usually recognized. Considerable gunnery work was done, especially during visits to Wheelus, and Lt Col Burns installed tracers to break his pilots of their tendency to fixate on their targets and press their strafing runs too close. To control the Voodoo as it passed through the 'corruption' from its own wildly

ricocheting tracers was a certain cure for the habit of shooting from too close.

Losses of the F-101A/C during the Bergstrom and Bentwaters years were higher than for many aircraft types but within reasonable limits. During its stay in the British Isles, the 81st TFW seems to have lost eight airplanes, which works out to roughly one per year. These include a machine lost during the December 1958 delivery, thought to be F-101C 56-0037. Another airframe, serial unknown, crashed on mud flats on approach to RAF Woodbridge on 13 February 1959 while yet another was lost at sea on 2 April 1959. In March 1962, F-101C 54-1491 was damaged and seems to have been written off. F-101C 56-0036 was lost on 19 December 1963 when pilot Major Bud Watt, making a landing approach at Bentwaters, apparently fell victim to the familiar pitch-up problem. Watt ejected safely but was hurt. Another aircraft, serial unknown but belonging to the wing's 78th TFS, was lost at Kettleburgh on 22 February 1964. F-101C 56-0012 crashed in the Fort William area on 7 May 1964. Finally, in October

1964, F-101A 54-1476 was observed in wrecked condition at Bentwaters. The last-named may have been the participant in a spectacular accident in which a Voodoo, its pilot already dead, ploughed into a building full of other pilots and set it afire.

Markings of the 81st TFW from December 1958 consisted of three styles each having two sunray streaks on the tail of the aircraft. Each squadron had its own colour, the 78th TFS having red, the 91st TFS blue, the 92nd TFS yellow. These colours also adorned the wingtips, tailplanes, wing fences and undercarriage door. Squadron badges were carried on the fin with wing badges below the cockpit. The commander of the wing, however, flew a machine which carried all three squadron badges and colours.

In 1961, a change brought Voodoo fins painted in one colour with thirteen stars superimposed on it, the colours being the same for each squadron. Main wheel doors also carried a single star in the centre, whilst squadron commanders had four stars on their wheel doors. In May 1962, in one of its periodic turnabouts, the US Air Force ruled that the airplanes

*Following its replacement at Bentwaters by the F-4C Phantom, this 81st TFW F-101A Voodoo (54-1475) has returned to Shaw AFB, South Carolina, where it was frozen, on 31 March 1966, in the camera lens of the inimitable Norman Taylor. Following their service as fighters, some F-101As were converted to RF-101G reconnaissance aircraft*
(Norman Taylor)

belonged to the wing rather than to squadrons. (This notion did not last long, but was resurrected in 1972). This ended individual squadron colours and meant that all three combined colours were applied to all aircraft of the 81st TFW.

The 81st TFW soldiered on with the Voodoo until 3 January 1966, when replacement of the type with the F-4C Phantom was completed and the final F-101A/C departed British soil. In recent months, a few examples—non-flyable—have returned, to be used for battle damage repair training.

## RF-101G/H Recce Voodoo

The final disposition of the surviving F-101A/C Voodoo airframes must be related a bit out of chronological sequence, and is actually a follow-up to the story of the reconnaissance Voodoo (next chapter).

Twenty-seven F-101A and thirty-four F-101C Voodoos were converted into reconnaissance airframes very late in their service lives and were employed briefly by the Air National Guard in Arkansas (154 TRS), Kentucky (165 TRS) and Nevada (192 TRS). Some reports give the figure for F-101C conversions as 29. The F-101A airframes became RF-101G aircraft, while the F-101C aircraft became RF-101H models. The conversion programme was under way when President Johnson activated ANG units on 28 January 1968 in response to heightened tensions in Korea which included an assassination attempt on President Park and the seizure of the US spy ship *Pueblo*. A massive show of US force was mounted, as tactical aircraft from various units in the US were rushed to the Korean peninsula or to nearby bases. The Voodoos, however, had not completed the conversion process and could not actually be deployed for a further six months.

Lt Col Donald J Lang of the 314th Air Division at Osan AB, Korea, who by 1968 had accumulated no fewer than two thousand hours in the Voodoo, wondered if the ANG RF-101G and RF-101H were the right machines for the job of deterring Pyongyang's adventurism. The author of this volume was in Seoul at the time and recalls that by then even the G and H models of the Voodoo seemed ancient.

The Arkansas ANG deployed twenty RF-101Gs to Itazuke AB near Fukuoka, Japan, with 'temporary' onward deployments to Osan. In November 1968, the Nevada ANG with RF-101Hs moved to Itazuke, allowing the Arkansas Voodoos to return stateside. In January 1969, the Kentucky ANG with RF-101Gs took over the Itazuke/Osan commitment, remaining until April. On 9 April 1969, with no way to know that a week later the North Koreans would shoot down an EC-121 Warning Star and kill 31 US Navy airmen, the new President, Richard Nixon, relieved the Air National Guardsmen of their active-duty commitment.

Eventually, the Nevada ANG relinquished its RF-101H aircraft to Kentucky and Kentucky shifted its RF-101Gs to Arkansas. These machines were retired in 1972, ending the service life of the single-seat F-101 Voodoo fighter, the orphan which ended up being adopted for the nuclear strike role and converted for the reconnaissance mission.

# Chapter 5
# The Fight by the Cotton Pickers
## Introducing the RF-101A Into Service

The Voodoo was the airplane flown by the first American squadron to go to war in Southeast Asia. Only the recce Voodoo saw combat. 'But my God, how those recce youngsters flew those RFs!' remembers Robin Olds, who had himself shifted by then to Phantoms (at Ubon). They *were* young, but most had served in Europe first and by the time they took the Voodoo into battle, they were old hands who flew and fought with unbridled tenacity. Says Olds, 'I had a standing order, no recce Voodoo jock could ever buy a drink at the Ubon bar . . .'

The brute power and long range which made the Voodoo an escort fighter and atomic bomber also rendered the airplane ideal as a dedicated recce platform. Originally, like the fighter Voodoo, the recce version was intended for SAC. McDonnell had studied an interchangeable nose for the F-88 to enable a single airframe to be field-modified for the photo mission, flying as an F-88A fighter on one sortie, an RF-88A reconnaissance craft the next. It was a good idea but it was forty years early. Today, recce squadron commanders like Lt Col Carl Loveland talk of a 'dial-a-plane' where the pilot can slip into his cockpit and choose the mission to be performed that day—a concept close to reality in the F-16 Fighting Falcon which can be 'podded' for the recce role. In the 1950s, it remained true that a tactical reconnaissance airplane performed no other mission with the special exception of the atomic strike role. The US Air Force's recce fleet consisted mostly of F-84F Thunderflashes—well-liked and widely used, but not expected to endure far beyond 1960.

The interchangeable nose idea was studied early in the F-101 programme but by 1953 it was clear that the Air Force wanted a dedicated recce Voodoo with no other role except that of carrying a centreline atomic bomb. On 11 October 1953, a letter of contract authorized McDonnell to reconfigure the 16th and 19th F-101As on the production line (54-149/150) and complete them as YRF-101A recce aircraft. On 13 January 1954 during an RF-101A mockup inspection (18 months after the mockup inspection of the basic F-101), it was decided to incorporate the bulky KA-1 camera (of which, more below), which in turn dictated the long, wedge-shaped configuration of the camera nose. The first YRF-101A was rolled out in May 1955 and flew on 30 June 1955. Not until December was the decision made that recce Voodoos would go not to SAC but to TAC. Some TAC officers complained that the RF-101A was no compensation for the RB-57 Canberra then being phased out of inventory (nor was it meant to be); it was also little consolation for the RF-104 and RF-105, both of which had been scratched from the Air Force's future reconnaissance forces. *Still* orphans in a sense, two YRF-101A prototypes were followed by 35 RF-101A airframes beginning with 54-1496, dubbed 'old 496' by men who flew it.

## Equipment

On a combat recce mission at low level which might last 3 hours 50 minutes, the RF-101A initially carried one 12-inch focal length Fairchild KA-2 framing camera shooting forward, three 6-inch focal length KA-2s in a forward tri-camera station shooting downward, and a pair of larger KA-1s farther arrears. A CAI KA-18 strip camera could be carried. A VF-31 viewfinder allowed the pilot to look 'through' the tri-camera station. Pilots liked many of the recce Voodoo's features, including its superb oxygen system and redundant flight refuelling ('flying boom' for the KC-97/KC-135 and 'probe and drogue' for the KB-50J), but the camera equipment was very different from that of the RF-84F and bringing it into service at the same time as a new airframe led to problems. The RF-101A was in fact ready for service before the fighter Voodoo and before its own cameras

*Originally the 16th F-101A on the production line and the first machine in the reconnaissance series (although delivered without cameras), YRF-101A Voodoo 54-149 is seen on a low-level flight near St Louis in May 1956. Pitot probe on port wingtip is not standard, and is presumably associated with early flight test programme (MDC)*

were ready. Without cameras, it joined the 363rd TRW under Brig Gen Stephen B Mack at Shaw AFB, SC, on 6 May 1957.

To continue on the subject of Voodoo recce equipment, in the late 1950s there were tests of an electronic strobe for night photo work during an exercise called 'Cloud Gap,' apparently related to President Eisenhower's proposal for an 'Open Skies' arrangement with the Soviet Union and conducted simultaneously with Exercise Desert Strike at Luke AFB, Arizona. The strobe created problems for pilots, with reflections disrupting night vision, and also led to reports of UFOs from Arizona to El Paso, Texas, during the period. Later, in Southeast Asia in the early 1960s, recce Voodoos were modified to carry photo flash cartridges and TLQ-8 jammers. The airplane's career Test Mod 1181, the 'Toy Tiger' update, was a complete retrofit of cameras introducing a new nose panoramic and 4.5 × 4.5-inch format KA-45s on side and vertical gyro stab, including night cameras using flash cartridges, as well as Hycon KS-72 cameras and automatic controls developed for the RF-4C Phantom.

The Voodoo's nose camera system had a battery-operated elevator to lower the camera to retrieve the film packs. When the cameras were not installed, the forward regions of the wedge-nosed Voodoo were

'Old 496' when new. The first production RF-101A
Voodoo (54-1496) in natural metal at the McDonnell St
Louis factory (note F3H-2N Demon in background). In
February 1957, this dedicated reconnaissance platform was
brand new and was viewed as a 'hot' century series jet. It
was not yet readily known that recce Voodoos would be
wearing warpaint
(MDC)

'Old 496' in battle paint. Although freshly painted in the
T.O.114 camouflage scheme which eventually became
standard in Southeast Asia, the first production RF-101A
Voodoo (54-1496), here at Shaw AFB, SC in 1968, is
about to be retired from service. A ceremony was planned
to send 'Old 496' off to the boneyard
(Lang)

LEFT
'Goodby [sic] 496, from all these people and many more who crewed you, flew you and knew you.' *Lt Col Donald J Lang points to the inscription on the first RF-101A (54-1496) which has been 'autographed' by numerous pilots who flew this Voodoo. Among signatures is one next to camera bay by Capt Pat Reaves, whose combat account appears in this narrative. 'Old 496' was being retired to the storage centre at Davis-Monthan AFB, Arizona*
(Lang)

'Old 496' in the boneyard. The first production RF-101A Voodoo (54-1496) at the Military Aircraft Storage and Disposition Center (MASDC), Davis-Monthan AFB, New Mexico, on 17 March 1969. The aircraft seems well preserved, but never flew again
(Douglas D Olson)

*RF-101A Voodoo (54-1513), probably at Kadena AB, Okinawa, where the 15th TRS (Cotton Pickers) was stationed in the early 1960s. Located beneath the 'R' in US AIR FORCE on this Voodoo is a cover for the pitch inhibitor. The aircraft also carries two 450-gal fuel tanks (USAF)*

LEFT
*The archetypical Voodoo pilot of the early 1960s. Captain Don Lang of the 29 TRS/363 TRW at Shaw AFB, South Carolina, prepares to go aboard his RF-101C (56-0188). Lang eventually logged 2,000 hours in the McDonnell airplane, at the end flying the Air National Guard RF-101G/Hs which went to Korea during the 1968 Pueblo crisis (courtesy Lt Col Lang)*

perfect for hauling cargo. On a flight from Kadena AB, Okinawa, to Hill AFB, Utah, a pilot carried a baby crib which astonished flight-line personnel when the elevator was lowered! Later, when a war was going on, a discriminating Voodoo pilot at Udorn brought a case of Moet et Chandom red Bordeaux wine to his Thai airbase from Guam in the camera compartment of a recce Voodoo.

In May 1957, Captain John R Evans went to Eglin AFB in the Florida panhandle to join the 3241st Test Squadron of the Air Research and Development Command (ARDC) to evaluate the RF-101A. Evans, soon to be in battle in a distant Asian country few Americans had heard of, joined the Voodoo programme when his assignment to the RF-104 and RF-105 died with those airplanes. He'd never flown a fast jet with afterburners and was required to log 'burner time in an F-100D Super Sabre before attempting to drive the Voodoo. The squadron had been given the first, third and fourth RF-101A airframes ('old 496,' 54-1498 and 54-1499). Major Daniel J (Jack) Nelson had ferried 54-1499 from St Louis to Eglin as a result of orders dated 2 May 1957 and Evans was scheduled to make his first flight in the machine on 13 May. When he taxied out, his yellow pitch inhibitor light blinked on, indicating that the 'stick knocker,' developed at such effort to resolve the pitch-up problem, was not working. A day later, the captain became a fully-fledged Voodoo pilot by taking an RF-101A up over Eglin's wet green swampland and out over the Gulf of Mexico.

In November 1957, Captain Donald J Lang was operations officer of the 4th Tow Target Squadron flying F/RF-80s and TB-26s when he first laid eyes on the airplane in which he would later log more than 2,000 hours. Captain Don Hawkins, a project officer on the upcoming RF-101A speed record attempt, Sun Run, had stopped at George AFB, Calif, to show off his new mount. Lang was impressed. 'It was huge, compared to my experience with RF-80, F-86 and WW 2 P-47. My first impression was that it represented a new generation of fighters—supersonic. It was *long*—I paced it off. I put in a request for RF-101A training . . .'

## Operation Sun Run

On 26 November 1957, an RF-101A Voodoo with pilot Gustave B Klatt set a west coast (Los Angeles to

New York to Los Angeles) transcontinental record of
6 hours, 42 min 6.9 seconds. On the return he set an
east-west record of 3 hours 34 mins 8.6 seconds. The
recce Voodoo was *fast* as well as long-legged, and very
young men in the 1950s were coming to love its brute
power and impressive speed. The 363rd TRW at
Shaw which flew the Voodoo in its 17th TRS and
18th TRS was soon joined by the 432nd TRW, which
was briefly a group before becoming a wing, initially
operating the 20th TRS and 29th TRS but eventually
acquiring all four squadrons.

The RF-101A was followed on the production line
by the RF-101C stressed for the higher gravity figure
and modified for the centreline nuclear weapon. The
RF-101C was first flown 12 July 1957. Following the
successful Sun Run undertaking, six RF-101As from
Shaw made a brief expedition outside to the western
Pacific in November 1957, reaching Guam, the
Philippines and Okinawa. Other 'RF' deployments
took place during the Formosa and Lebanon crises.
The recce Voodoo was introduced to the Pacific
region in early 1959 when the 15th TRS (the Cotton
Pickers) at Kadena AB, Okinawa, and the 45th TRS
(the Polka Dots) at Misawa AB, Japan, transitioned
from RF-84F to RF-101C. In May 1958, the Shaw-
based 17th TRS and 18th TRS were shifted to
France, becoming part of the 66th TRW at Laon AB,
France. At Shaw, there came into being the 4414th
Combat Crew Training Squadron (CCTS) to train
recce Voodoo pilots. Thus, Shaw had the 20th TRS,
29th TRS and 4414th CCTS; Laon was now
headquarters for the 17th TRS, 18th TRS, 32nd
TRS and 38th TRS, and the Western Pacific
accomodated the 15th TRS and 45th TRS. The
Cotton Pickers were going to be heard from again.

## Chinese RF-101As

Under Operation Boom Town, RF-101A Voodoos
were secretly delivered to the Chinese Nationalist Air
Force, which finally acknowledged this at a Taipei
news conference on 29 October 1959. Chiang Kai-
shek's regime on Formosa insisted that the Voodoos
were being used only for coastal flights over
international waters. In fact, the Nationalists pene-
trated airspace over the mainland in every manner of
recce machine from the B-17G Flying Fortress to the
U-2. In March 1965, Peking media credited Chinese
communist pilot Kao Chang-chi with shooting down

*Over Florence, SC, RF-101C Voodoo 56-176 of the 29
TRS moves up to refuel from a KB-50J Superfortress. On
a night refuelling, Lt Col Donald J Lang pushed the hose
up too far and found himself reading the words, 'Hughes
Aircraft, Birmingham, Alabama,' inside the drogue
housing. Wingman Lt William Kirk very calmly chided,
'Don, I think you're too close.' Kirk downed two MiGs in
Vietnam and now commands TAC's Ninth Air Force
(courtesy Lt Col Lang)*

an RF-101A over China. Peking also claimed the capture of a Voodoo pilot, Major Hseih Hsing-ho, in December 1964. John Evans remembers a ferry flight eastward across the Pacific to *return* two ex-Nationalist RF-101As to US inventory, and recalls that the airplanes had no markings of any kind, but his records do not reveal dates or serial numbers.

Captain Robert D Caudry, another of the many Voodoo men who later became a general, was one of the instructor pilots in the 15th TRS assigned to train the Chinese. He had one of the Chinese pilots instruct him on what to say in the Chinese *language* to a controller on a flying visit to Formosa. Bob Caudry uttered the radio message with careful attention to the strict demands of a tonal language only to be greeted by mute silence from the control tower. He found out that the message he'd relayed in flawless Chinese was, 'Look out below, I'm coming in for a very bad landing.' Today, the only relic of at least a half-dozen years of clandestine Voodoo intrusions into China is the display RF-101A Voodoo (54-1505) located at the new museum at Taipei airport and painted in a camouflage scheme never employed operationally.

## RF-101A/C in France

If Waterloo was won on the playing fields of Eton, the battle for the skies over North Vietnam was shaped by the men who flew Voodoos at low level and high speed across the hills and hedgerows of the European plain. While Kadena's 15th TRS Cotton Pickers trained Chinese pilots and also began flying combat support missions in and around Vietnam in sanitized RF-101A/Cs (no markings or uniforms)—operating from Tan Son Nhut AB, Saigon, beginning in October 1961 under the code name Pipe Stem (later Able Mabel)—the real 'action' was in Europe.

The 66th TRW at Laon AB, France, developed a cadre of reconnaissance pilots who were the best in

the world at low-level, high-speed recce and nuclear delivery missions. Voodoo pilots memorized the patchwork quilt of Europe. Eventually, the Laon-based 66th TRW had squadrons at Phalsbourg and Ramstein. Its pilots, like those operating Voodoo fighters during the same period, were the best in the Air Force.

Major Daniel J (Jack) Nelson had the job most fighter pilots wanted—command of a squadron—and remembers it well:

'When Bert Grigsby was killed night flying in an RF-84F at Phalsbourg, Colonel Bob Gideon [Robert R Gideon, Jr], wing commander, sent me down to take the 38th TRS. The 32nd TRS was the other squadron at Phalsbourg, wing headquarters and two further squadrons remaining at Laon. I had to get recurrent and fly the RF-84F for a couple of months before my RF-101s started arriving. I flew with the 32nd a couple of times to maintain my RF-101

RIGHT
*In the late 1950s and early 1960s, the playing fields of Europe provided advanced learning for young, skilled RF-101C Voodoo pilots who would take their aircraft to war a continent away. RF-101C Voodoo (56-0226) of the 66th Tactical Reconnaissance Wing, flying over France in the early 1960s*
*(Courtesy MSGT Kenneth R Fox)*

BELOW
*Wearing USAF serial 54-1505 and Chinese Nationalist number 5660, this RF-101A Voodoo sits on outdoor display at Taipei Airport today. It is not really known whether this aircraft is, in fact, 54-1505, or whether it served operationally with the Chinese. RF-101A Voodoos operated from Formosa in the 1950s were not camouflaged and not much was said about them*
*(Andy Heap)*

currency and, while flying with them, discovered that I might have a problem transitioning *my* squadron into the Voodoo.

'The IPs [instructor pilots] for the 32nd acted like they were afraid of the airplane and were flying it like a bomber. They were teaching huge "cross-country type" landing patterns. I got *my* IPs together and we taught fighter patterns and aerodynamic braking. The 101 is the best airplane I've ever seen for aerodynamic braking (it has so much flat surface underneath that it really slows down rapidly during the landing roll). I tried unsuccessfully a couple of times to get the handbook changed to take advantage of these characteristics. I also got in trouble with my boss, Col Jerry Brown, the wing DO [deputy for operations] when I convinced him that aerodynamic

LEFT
*RF-101C Voodoo (56-0049) of 66th TRW, home based in Laon, France, meeting up with KC-135A Stratotanker (63-8021) over NATO skies*
(Col H Tiffault via Norman Taylor)

*This RF-101C Voodoo (56-0099), known as 'Balls 99,' was the personal mount of Major Daniel J (Jack) Nelson, commander of the 38th TFS at Phalsbourg AB, France, in 1959. The squadron, which had a nuclear strike role in addition to its reconnaissance function, later moved to Ramstein AB, Germany, but remained under the 66th Tactical Reconnaissance Wing headquartered at Laon AB, France*
(courtesy Col D J Nelson)

braking was the only way to land on Europe's short and often wet runways. He proceeded to drag the afterburners on one of his next few flights.

'Speaking of wet runways, we had a heck of a time convincing people that we had a tyre problem. The F-100 had always had a problem with tyres blowing on takeoff with heavy loads (which created long takeoff rolls and consequently a lot of heat on the tyres). So the 'dimple' tyre was developed for century series aircraft. It solved the F-100's takeoff problem but when we started getting them in our inventory I got a rash of airplanes in the barrier [making emergency arrests] so I told my maintenance people to [get rid of] those tyres. Subsequent tests showed that the 'dimple' tyres had only 15 per cent of the braking capability of ribbed tyres on wet runways.

'In Europe, a high percentage of flying is IFR [instrument flight rules] so the autopilot was a great instrument. As an old fighter pilot who had been hand-flying an airplane for 15 years, I thought the autopilot was the best invention since sliced bread. However, I had some young pilots who weren't that enthused, claiming that they had turned on the autopilot and had been flipped upside down. I told them I didn't believe that, and that if I flew an airplane with the autopilot out I was going to find out who flew the previous flight and [why he] didn't write it up.

'One night while we were night-flying, "Scotty" Wetzel came in for his landing [at Phalsbourg]. The mobile control officer noticed that he was crossing the end of the runway about to touch down, so the mobile control officer turned on his flashlight to log the time.

He heard two afterburners light and looked up to see the Voodoo backing vertically into the ground with both afterburners going. At landing weight there is an almost one-to-one thrust/weight ratio, so he backed into the ground relatively softly. Scotty wasn't hurt but the ride was so terrifying that he doesn't remember anything after starting his go-around. Anyway, as a result of Scotty's accident plus the fact that Bert Grigsby had been killed landing on that runway (the approach came down the side of a hill with no approach lights which created an optical illusion of the runway standing on end until you crossed the end of the runway) I told Operations that any time the wind was such that we'd have to use that runway, to cancel night flying. Some of the junior types in Wing Ops told me I couldn't cancel flying because of wind direction but Colonel [Kyle L] Riddle [who'd replaced Colonel Robert R Gideon, Jr as wing commander, although Nelson is wrong about his rank; Riddle was a brigadier general] backed me completely. I lost two other 101s during my tour as commander of the 28th TRS but never lost a pilot. I had eleven bachelors in that squadron and they were a crazy bunch of *good pilots*.'

One 66th TRW squadron, the 38th TRS, moved from France to Ramstein AB, Germany—but *not*, as has been reported elsewhere, because of the recce bird's secondary nuclear strike mission. In fact, although France would not allow foreign nuclear weapons on her soil, all four of the 66th TRW squadrons, including the three which remained in France, trained for the atomic delivery function. Stirling: 'A contingency plan existed to deliver the weapons to Laon AB under specified circumstances and our certified crews were assigned targets.' Another flier with the 66th TRW shortly after Nelson's time notes that the RF-101C's additional nuclear strike mission with a 3,000-lb (1359-kg) Mark 7 atomic bomb on the centreline (a mission never assigned the RF-101A) impeded the 38th TRS's efforts to remain effective in the reconnaissance role. Despite the mission, and bombs being available to bases in France, *no Voodoo ever actually flew with an atomic bomb aboard*. Indeed, it seems likely that no single-seat fighter ever did, for 'failsafe' precautions and rules of engagement prevented it. Jack Nelson and other Voodoo pilots *did* deploy from Laon, Phalsbourg and Ramstein to Wheelus to 'work out' with mock nuclear shapes, however.

## Colonel McCartan's Flying

Colonel Arthur A McCartan honed his skills on the recce Voodoo criss-crossing Europe's hedgerows with the 66th TRW at Laon, 1958–61, then moved to Shaw AFB to take command of the 363rd TRW from 1 September 1961 to 19 August 1963. This put him in charge of the wing during the head-to-head confrontation over Cuba (of which, more soon). Every pilot had a pitch-up story, of course—simply reiterating that the Voodoo was a finely-tooled machine of great power never satisfies the listener—and McCartan's begins with another scrape with France's *l'Armee de l'Air*.

'Two RF-101Cs were slowing up preparing to start down an approach chute from 30,000 ft [9144 m]. This was in April 1961 near Rheims, France, and they were headed toward Laon airbase. Two French fighters jumped them, dragging their shadows across the formation. Lead RF-101C says, "Let's go get 'em!" He pushed up the throttles, brought in his speed brakes, and turned to keep the French in sight. BANG, he has pitched up!

'The wingman continued to fly around Lead, offering advice. Lead tried all the cures for pitch-up—stick forward, drag chute out, full throttle, afterburner, rudders neutral, etc. Nothing worked. The RF-101C was falling at 5,000 ft [1524 m] per minute—airspeed flopping between 50 and 100 knots [160 and 210 km/h], nose slowly turning. The controls had no effect, yet at times Lead said, "I think I've got it." Plenty of time to try everything. The wingman commanding, "EJECT!" as the aircraft settled below 20,000 ft [6096 m]. More commands, "EJECT, EJECT!" and finally Lead ejects near 10,000 ft [3048 m]. In the calm conditions the aircraft, seat, canopy and pilot land close to each other (100–200 yards) [90–180 m]. The aircraft landed flat with underbelly depressing the French clay field about 6 inches or so. Tail broke slightly with twisted drag chute draped over it. Windscreen and aft permanent canopy uncracked. There was no fire. The point is that the pilot (combat qualified) had no idea he was putting the aircraft into a critical aerodynamic situation. Once in it, he was positive he was regaining control and calmly trying everything as he was coming straight down. The aircraft stayed flat throughout the fall.'

## The Cotton Pickers

'*The 15th Tactical Reconnaissance Squadron is an intelligence collection agency, and performing its combat mission the jocular phrase "Kill 'em with film" becomes a reality, for indirectly our pilots do exactly that with hostile forces. At present the mission is supported by the "long bird," the McDonnell-built RF-101 Voodoo, a dependable, twin-jet aircraft capable of generating more than 30,000 pounds [13,607 kg] of thrust and climbing its 25 tons [22,680 kg] eight miles up [12,874 m] in less than 150 seconds.*'

So wrote Major Alexander P Butterfield in February 1963, when he commanded the 15th TRS (the Cotton Pickers) at Kadena AB, Okinawa. From 1961, the squadron's Voodoos were flying combat missions in Laos and South Vietnam in the 'Pipe Stem/Able Mabel' commitment—first from Saigon's Tan Son Nhut, later from Bangkok's Don Muang Airport. Alex Butterfield is best remembered as the Appointments Secretary in the Nixon White House

staff who, in 1973, revealed that the President's conversations were being recorded on the Watergate Tapes, but a decade earlier Butterfield was an able Voodoo flier and natural leader.

The Cotton Pickers were commanded by Major Russel E Oakes (1960) and Lt Col Earl A Butts (1960–62) before Butterfield took the helm (1963). Don Lang, who served in the squadron under all three, believes that one of its saddest moments came *before* the onset of war. In the fall of 1960, Captain Charles Lavender was flying an RF-101 out of Korea to Japan. He had an engine fire, ejected, and was seen by his circling wingman to get into his inflated raft only to be pulled out by his chute in the water—like a sea anchor. Lavender drowned.

At Eglin, Jack Nelson drew the job of giving Butterfield his first checkout in a Voodoo. Nelson was told to give the squadron commander-to-be in 10 days the transition which normally took eight weeks. No problem, except that on his first solo ride in an F-101B, the actuator on Butterfield's nose gear door sheared and the nose gear refused to come down. 'Alex was a good pilot and we briefed him to make a normal landing, holding the nose off as long as possible and then lowering it onto a strip of foam we had laid on the runway.' Butterfield made a perfect landing but the incident caused an orderly room clerk to discover that the future Cotton Pickers commander did not have records with him. Major General Gordon M Graham, DO of Tactical Air Command, had to intercede to persuade the desk-pusher that Nelson was *supposed* to train Butterfield.

*In the 'Cotton Pickers' standard markings employed in Okinawa, Korea, and initially Southeast Asia—replete with commander's stripe around mid-fuselage—Major Donald J Lang flies 15th TRS RF-101C (56-0227) (courtesy Lt Col Lang)*

BELOW
*Although in no way involved in the questionable practices of the Watergate period, Alexander Butterfield is best remembered as the White House official who in 1973 revealed the existence of the Nixon tapes. In October 1962, Lt Col Butterfield [left] commanded the 15th TRS 'Cotton Pickers' at Kadena AB, Okinawa, and was already sending RF-101C Voodoo detachments to Southeast Asia (courtesy Lt Col John R Evans)*

ABOVE
*Previously published but once in a historical journal and credited to 'photographer unknown,' this cluttered shot of a 15th TRS 'Cotton Pickers' RF-101C Voodoo (56-0049) was taken by a 19-year-old enlisted airman during an Armed Forces Day display at Osan AB, Korea, in May 1960. Squadron pilot Captain Charles Lavender was lost near Korea soon afterward, and the tail markings (yellow and black squares, red lightning bolt) were shed when the squadron began its 1961 move to Southeast Asia*
(Robert F Dorr)

LEFT
*A2C Robert F Dorr, age 19, stands beneath tail of 'Cotton Pickers' 15th TRS RF-101C Voodoo (56-0049) at Osan AB, Korea, in May 1959. The Voodoos prowled the Korean Demilitarized Zone, obtaining oblique photography of communist preparations above the 38th Parallel. Soon afterward, the Okinawa-based squadron sent Voodoos to Southeast Asia*
(Robert F Dorr)

John Evans was one of the first Americans to take the Voodoo to war. The Able Mabel detachment of the 15th TRS was operating from Don Muang airfield (Bangkok International Airport) when Evans took three RF-101C Voodoos in. The Kennedy administration had made a commitment to keep tabs on the communist Pathet Lao in Laos, who were receiving Soviet economic and military help. In addition, having begun to supply B-26 and T-28 aircraft to next-door South Vietnam, the Kennedy advisors were interested in recce photos of operations by the Viet Cong. Because so many of them had flown in Europe, Evans and his cohorts had an average age of 31 to 35, and an average of 1,500 hours fast-jet time, most of it in the Voodoo. At Don Muang, they developed their film after dark to avoid attention. While considerable risk emanated from Pathet Lao gunfire—pilot Don O'Meara was hit by Triple-A over the Plaine des Jarres and crash-landed, though both he and his Voodoo survived—the men also worried about being attacked by cobras while pacing towards the photo facility after dark. Most were glad when they moved back to Tan Son Nhut, where the Voodoo pilots had a seven-bedroom French villa, no cobras, housegirls, but no washing machine.

In aircraft 54-1499 on 7 July 1962, John Evans was over the Plaine des Jarres when he spotted two aircraft similar to the C-47 but with CCCP (actually SSSR, in Cyrillic) painted on them. These were Ilyushin Il-14 cargo craft and the much-needed proof that the Pathets were being directly supplied by the Russians. Evans' Voodoo film of this discovery was regarded as so important that it was processed hastily and rushed to Washington the same day via B-57.

Having staked out their turf in South Vietnam, the Cotton Pickers were in the war to stay at a time when most Americans were looking for trouble in a different direction—from Fidel Castro. On early combat missions, Evans' RF-101s were refuelled by US Navy A4D-2 Skyhawks carrying 'buddy' refuelling packs, since no Air Force tankers were readily available. When F-102 Delta Daggers of the 555th TFS were brought in to share their berth at Tan Son Nhut, the Voodoo pilots were determined to keep the best parking areas for themselves. The F-102 leader insisted that higher headquarters wanted *his* fighters to have the best parking revetments and demanded that the Voodoos be removed. Evans promptly replied that they were in Saigon with South Vietnamese permission and that only a native officer, Colonel Tri, could authorize the aircraft parking change. The F-102 people searched diligently for Colonel Tri while their delta fighters sat forlorn in the boondocks. They never did obtain the South Vietnamese colonel's permission, the Voodoos retained the preferred parking spaces, and years later Evans confided to a Dagger pilot that Colonel Tri had been a figment of Evans' own imagination!

The Vietnam war was under way—although the public scarcely knew yet and years would pass before Voodoos pointed their noses towards North Vietnam. Meanwhile, by September 1962, Nikita Khruschev was doing his best to sneak strategic missiles into Cuba under Jack Kennedy's nose. Cuba? With the Pathet Lao shooting at *them*, the Cotton Pickers had no idea why two of their best airplanes, those with the 'Toy Tiger' mod, were flown *back* to the US for missions against Cuba. In September 1962, the important bird probing Castroland was the U-2, not the RF-101A/C, and the term Cuban Missile Crisis had not yet been invented.

## Cuban Missile Crisis

Moscow's attempt to place missiles in the Western Hemisphere and alter the world balance of power was discovered by U-2 overflights. Kennedy and his advisors, including Defense Secretary McNamara and Secretary of State Rusk, agonized over the evidence before concluding that a stand had to be made. Vast numbers of men and machines were moved to the southern extremity of the US, some at Key West only 90 miles (144 km) from Cuba, for the October 1962 confrontation. The Voodoo joined the U-2 in surveilling the Soviet build up.

Jack Nelson commanded the 4414th Combat Crew Training Squadron (CCTS), part of Arthur McCartan's 363rd TRW, at Shaw. Nelson was playing golf, a pastime common among Voodoo pilots, on a Sunday afternoon. The training group personnel officer told Nelson to round up all his pilots

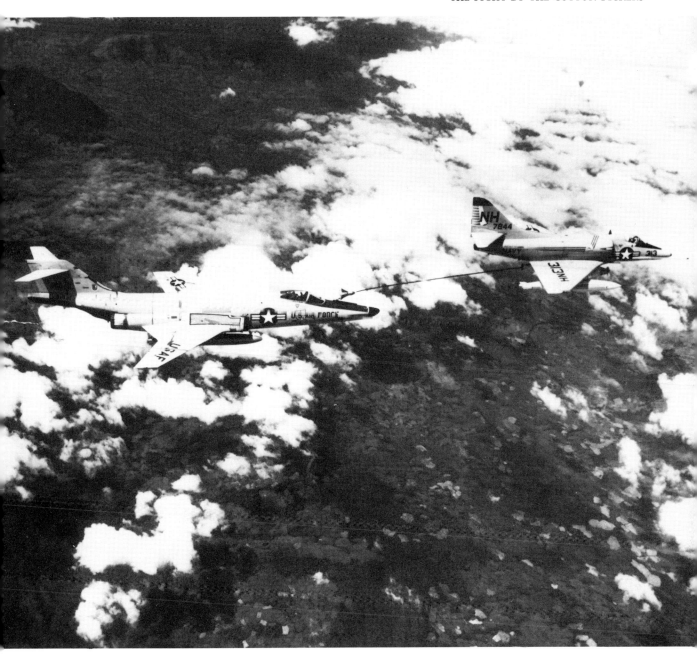

*The beginning of the Southeast Asia commitment. Still with colourful tail markings, recce Voodoos of the Cotton Pickers are inspected by the King and Queen of Thailand and the Thai chief of staff, at Bangkok's Don Muang Airport. Captain Art Gould (in flight suit) stands in front of RF-101C Voodoo (56-0047) which will later be hit by Pathet Leo ground fire and returned to the 4416th Test Squadron at Shaw*
(courtesy Lt Col Donald J Lang)

*Because they were the first US Air Force squadron to operate in the Southeast Asia conflict, the 'Cotton Pickers' of the 15th TRS had no in-theatre tanker support for their missions over Laos and South Vietnam. Throughout much of the early 1960s, the only air-refuelling tankers available were US Navy carrier-based Skyhawks, like this A-4C from USS* Kitty Hawk *(CVA-63)*
(courtesy John Lewis)

(except the one RAF exchange officer assigned to the squadron) and have them packed and ready to move to MacDill AFB, Florida. A lot of pilots and planes went to Florida that month. Though Nelson's was the RTU (replacement training unit), many of his pilots were integrated into the wing's other tactical squadrons and began flying missions south to Castroland, thumbing their afterburners at Fidel's MiG-17s and Triple-A. Because he was assigned to a command-post job, Nelson got to make only one flight over Cuba.

Any doubt that this was serious business was dispelled when a U-2 was shot down and its pilot killed. One night when going over the frag order (mission order), Nelson noticed that he was fragged (assigned) to send an RF-101 over a camouflaged Russian-Cuban site—at low level, supersonic—*to knock down the camouflage netting with the plane's supersonic boom*!

'I called TAC to tell them that they had lost their minds. In the first place, a shock wave from a sonic boom would have little or no effect on anything as porous as camouflaged netting. Secondly, the skin on the 101 fuselage "oil-canned" and, as we learned in Europe during Royal Flush [an annual NATO recce competition], this oil-canning at high speed and high "Q" [air density] caused the airplane to shed large chunks of skin. The duty officer at TAC assured me that General [Walter C] Sweeney [TAC commander] had ordered the mission. I said if he really wanted to try it he should send an F-104 which we learned at Eglin could fly supersonic at sea level as smoothly as subsonic. Anyway, the whole mission got scrubbed.'

Though it was a deadly 'eyeball-to-eyeball' confrontation which brought the world perilously close to nuclear war, the Cuban Missile Crisis—managed direct from the White House by Kennedy, McNamara, Rusk and others—was not resolved without considerable reliance upon symbols. With Jack Kennedy living at 1600 Pennsylvania Avenue, it could have been no coincidence that the first US Navy vessel to send a boarding party to a Russian ship heading into Cuba was the destroyer USS *Joseph P Kennedy* (DD-850), named after the President's deceased older brother. (*Kennedy*, whose skipper had the unlikely name Nicholas Mikhalevsky, accompanied USS *John R Pierce* (DD-753) to intercept and board the SS *Marucla* at 0642 hours on 26 October 1962, the first time American sailors boarded a hostile vessel in the twentieth century). With a naval officer, Admiral Robert L Dennison, commanding Atlantic Fleet forces, it was no accident that the first tactical reconnaissance missions over the island were flown by RF-8A Crusaders (known as F8U-1P until the previous month) on 23 October 1962. With the Strategic Air Command dominant within the US Air Force, it was certainly no fluke that U-2s continued to make high-altitude photo flights over the Russian medium-range ballistic missile installations in Cuba,

even after the 27 October 1962 shoot-down by an SA-2 missile which resulted in the death of pilot Captain Rudolph Anderson. RF-101A/C pilots, many of whom were far more experienced than the RF-8A or U-2 jocks, sat on the ground at MacDill and, for the first few days of the unfolding crisis, twiddled their thumbs. The Voodoo pilots were perhaps the only men in American uniform to have perfected low-level recce flying—a generation ahead of their time—and some were almost blind with rage that their talents weren't being employed.

Once the RF-101A/C Voodoo airmen were turned loose, they flew eighty-two combat missions over Cuba between 26 October and 15 November, many in the face of anti-aircraft fire. Denouement of the crisis came on 29 October when Khruschev 'blinked,' as Rusk later put it, and bowed to American demands to remove his missiles.

Although the outcome of the confrontation was viewed at the time as an American victory (if a guarantee not to invade the island was the price for withdrawal of the missiles, that *quid pro quo* was not publicized), it was a far from gratifying experience for most of the RF-101 pilots. Few got to fly more than a mission or two over Fidel Castro's terrain, and some experienced nothing more exciting than going from MacDill to the Florida keys only as a 'spare,' to turn around and head home while a wingman went in. The Voodoos were in a top state of maintenance, the men were up, and they *wanted* to fly. They took pride in being able to fly and fight as low as 100 ft (30.4 m) off the ground, far beneath the operating envelope of the SA-2 missile. Though most of the pilots had come only as far as the distance from Shaw, as has been noted, a couple of the RF-101s at MacDill during the crisis had actually been withdrawn from Southeast Asia. With everybody thinking that a world war was about to explode around them, with a mission waiting to be performed and no one able to do the job better, the Voodoo pilots itched to fly and fight—and had not nearly enough opportunity.

A few F-101B two-seat, dual-control equipment airplanes, sometimes called F-101F (next chapter), were operated by reconnaissance units at various times in the Voodoo's history so that crews could transition more easily. Virginia Biggins of the Newport News, Virginia *Daily Press* was one of the first females to fly in a Voodoo in January 1963 when Jack Nelson of the 4414th CCTS at Shaw took her for a ride. Miss Biggins praised the 363rd TRW and commander McCartan and pointed out that the wing's achievements during the Cuban Missile Crisis hadn't been easy. 'In a matter of seconds, the time it takes to fly over a target area, the pilot must establish the kind of material that went into building a bridge, its length, height, number of beams, and numerous other peculiarities. A typical mission, to photograph a dam-powerplant complex, certain bridges and an airfield can be a challenge to a pilot's skills.'

## Voodoo in Europe

Once Cuba faded from the headlines and Southeast Asia returned to the back burner, the place to fly the recce Voodoo was, once again, Europe. A sage squadron commander finally persuaded higher-ups that the nuclear bomb mission assigned to the recce Voodoo was nonsensical and that it degraded the reconnaissance capabilities of his pilots, so it was dropped. RF-101C Voodoo pilots based in Europe took top honours in their first appearance at the 'William Tell' worldwide weapons meet at Nellis AFB, Nevada, in September 1962, and also appeared regularly at NATO Royal Flush competitions which tested all types of reconnaissance aircraft.

## Southeast Asia

By 1962, the Cotton Pickers of the 15th TRS were firmly entrenched in Southeast Asia. The Polka Dots of the 45th TRS, still headquartered at Misawa AB, Japan, also sent rotational pilots and airplanes. Major Butterfield once remarked that the Voodoo mission, still directed primarily against the Pathet Lao, was 'one of the toughest jobs I know.' The 'Toy Tiger' airplanes of the 15th TRS, the same machines temporarily moved stateside during the Cuban

*RF-101C Voodoo of the 18th TRS flies over Stonehenge in England in early 1969*
*(Gustafson)*

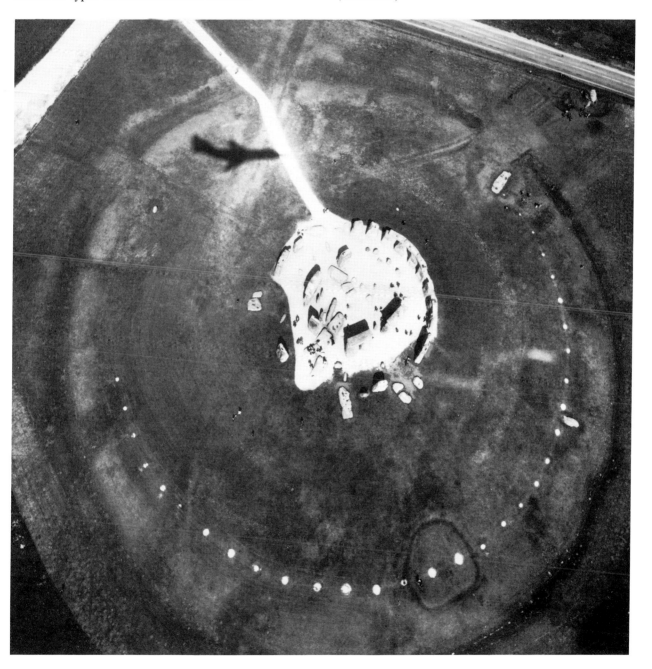

Missile Crisis, were the first reconnaissance aircraft able to function regularly at night, though the nighttime flash cartridges often confused and disoriented the RF-101C pilot, requiring him to carry out a mission against rag-tag guerrillas solely on instruments. On 6 November 1962, flights over Laos were temporarily discontinued (until 1 May 1964) but by now the Cotton Pickers and the Polka Dots were operating regularly against the Viet Cong from Tan Son Nhut AB, where on 1 April 1963 the size of the Voodoo detachment was increased from four to six aircraft. Two more airplanes remained at Don Muang to support the Thais against a little-publicized insurgency in their own country.

In 1963, the 2nd Air Division was established at Tan Son Nhut as headquarters for US Air Force units in South Vietnam. It was to be expanded and to become Seventh Air Force a couple of years later. Storm clouds were darkening. The 45th TRS took over the 'Able Mabel' RF-101C commitment at Tan Son Nhut for a time, and Composite Strike Force 'One Buck' sent six more RF-101Cs from Shaw to reinforce the 15th TRS, which rejoined 'Able Mabel' when the Voodoo operation was increased to twelve airplanes. No one could have failed to know that expansion of the American role in the small, tough war was under consideration. A 1964 White Paper

issued by Rusk's Department of State, *Aggression From the North*, made the argument that the communist insurgencies in Laos and South Vietnam were being steered from Hanoi. This was not yet entirely true, but it soon would be. Meanwhile, experiments were being conducted with camouflage well in advance of worldwide Air Force usage of camouflage colours. At least a half-dozen variations were tried as early as 1964, and the recce Voodoos did not settle into the 'final' Southeast Asia T.O.114 camouflage scheme until at least late 1964. A further year would pass before Voodoos began to acquire two-letter tailcodes then coming into Air Force use.

## Wider War

In the months after President Kennedy's assassination, the idea of increasing the US role in Vietnam had been vigorously debated along with the even more attractive idea—to the Joint Chiefs of Staff (JCS), at least—of carrying the war to North Vietnam. Although American soldiers were dying in combat on the ground in their 'advisory' role, North Vietnam had as yet been untouched by the US war machine.

A plan drawn up and approved by the JCS on 17 April 1964 contained a list of 94 targets in North

Vietnam which would collapse under the weight of US airpower in a matter of days, it was said, if only US warplanes could be sent against the North. In the 1964 election campaign, American voters understood that candidate Senator Barry Goldwater wanted to bomb North Vietnam while incumbent Lyndon Johnson did not. Having spoken to Goldwater during a 1964 campaign breakfast at San Francisco International Airport, the author is not so certain that the Senator wanted to bomb the North any more than the President did. Goldwater, however, had personally flown everything from the P-47 Thunderbolt to the F-4 Phantom and knew his subject. Clearly, he understood that an aerial campaign against Hanoi, if unleashed, would have to be total. Halfway measures would only ensnarl the Americans in a prolonged and unsatisfactory fight, with casualties that the public back home would not accept.

Even when North Vietnamese torpedo boats attacked US vessels in the Gulf of Tonkin on 2 August 1964, President Johnson authorized only *ad hoc* retaliation in the form of a single day's combat missions, although these resulted in the first death and the first capture of an American pilot up North. Viet Cong attacks against the south, including a savage mortar attack on US men and aircraft at Bien Hoa airbase in November 1964, heightened the

feeling that the war had to be turned towards North Vietnam on a sustained basis. Bombing the North would end the war within days, one general said. McNamara said that the US-supported regime in Saigon was growing stronger (it wasn't) and that where a US role in the conflict was concerned, he could see the light at the end of the tunnel.

That light did not exist.

Voodoos were going to have to go north.

Just a few days before 13 February 1965, when Johnson authorized the sustained assault on North Vietnam which became known as Rolling Thunder, two Voodoo pilots sat on jerrycans near runway's end at Tan Son Nhut, aware that the airfield could be mortared at any time. They looked at each other. Cotton Pickers, Polka Dots—and soon, Green Pythons—were by far the most experienced of American combat pilots. Perhaps, too, they were the most prescient. Now their small backwater war with its combat interspaced between sessions with women and booze in Saigon was losing its romantic, Hemingway appeal—if, indeed it had ever had such appeal. Vietnam would not, for much longer, be an obscure name in American geography lessons. One of the pilots inserted a blade of elephant grass between his teeth, beckoned out toward Tan Son Nhut's increasingly busy parking apron, and raised an eyebrow.

'You know what?' he said. 'We could even end up flying to Hanoi.'

'Naw. They're gonna pull us out of here. This place isn't that important.'

'I don't think so.' Pipe Stem and Able Mabel had lasted from 1961 to 1965. 'I don't think we're at the end, pal. I think we're at the beginning. I think some of us are going to see Hanoi from the air.'

On 6 May 1965, Captain Robert A Stubberfield of the Polka Dots, in an RF-101C Voodoo (56-0045) went deep into North Vietnam and was shot down by Hanoi's fast-growing anti-aircraft arsenal, the first Voodoo pilot to be killed in action.

*Lt Col A Robert Gould was with the first Americans who took Voodoos into South Vietnam in 1961. Much later, Gould was serving with the 17th TRS at RAF Upper Heyford, England, and flying over Spain when he tangled with the two-seat recce aircraft that would eventually replace his RF-101C. Gould's explanation of these three photos? 'I jumped an RF-4C during fair weather flying over Seville, Spain, winter 1968. I lost. The RF-4C took these pics!'*
*(A Robert Gould)*

# Chapter 6
# The Defence of the American Continent
## Manning the F-101B On Alert

It exists no longer but in its heyday Air Defense Command (ADC) was one of the largest components of the US Air Force, fielding as many as fifty fighter squadrons to defend North America from Soviet bombers. The range and power of the Voodoo made it a natural to intercept Russian bombers as far from North American cities as possible, but in October 1952 an ADC feeler toward an interceptor Voodoo was given the thumbs-down because of cost. ADC kept up the pressure. A paper competition for a new interceptor, completed in June 1954, pitted the intended Voodoo against the North American F-100B Super Sabre and the unbuilt Northrop F-89F Scorpion. The North American product, redesignated YF-107A, ended up being a fighter-bomber instead and in February 1955 a contract was finally let for the winning Voodoo interceptor. A little-known fact uncovered by historian Fred Roos is that in the spring of 1955, the Air Force intended to call the interceptor Voodoo the F-109. Reports of the F-109 designation being applied to Bell and Ryan designs are inaccurate. The decision to make the Voodoo a two-seater and to order 651 of them was made when the designation F-101B was assigned in August 1955.

The spectre of Soviet bombers carrying out transpolar attacks against US cities was regarded with the utmost seriousness. In 1954, the author watched Soviet air attachés gawking at a bomb-delivery demonstration by a B-47 Stratojet at Bolling Field in Washington, DC. Moscow lost no time in showing off its own bombers. On Soviet Aviation Day in July 1955, USAF Chief of Staff General Nathan F Twining and other westerners reported seeing ten Myasishchyev M-4 *Bison* bombers flying by, then nine more and nine more again. In fact, the *same* M-4s flew three times across the reviewing stand, but Air Force generals told budgetmakers that Russia's bomber fleet would be twice the size of SAC's by 1959. This 'bomber gap' was nonsense, like

the 'missile gap' which put Jack Kennedy in the White House in 1960, but there *was* a threat. In an odd incident in 1959, sixteen Tupolev Tu-16 *Badger-B* bombers actually carrying atomic bombs took off from a base in the eastern USSR and orbited over the Sea of Japan for several hours, intentions unknown, before being recalled. The F-101B, with impressive ordnance and endurance, *was* needed.

In May 1956, the interceptor was delayed by a production 'hold' and the number of airframes to be procured was reduced to 479. Budgetary and technical delays impeded progress with the # 1 airframe and McDonnell decided to complete it as the sole 6.33G-limited two-seater, designated NF-101B (56-0232). On 27 March 1957, this first Voodoo interceptor finally went aloft at St Louis with Bob Little on board.

## Equipment

Because it was designed to intercept bombers, the F-101B was a different Voodoo. Its forward fuselage had tandem pressurized and air-conditioned cockpits under a single clamshell-style plexiglass canopy, opened and closed by an electric actuator. The F-101B was heavier than single-seat Voodoos and employed larger tyres with a beefed-up undercarriage and bulges in the lower gear doors and undersides of the fuselage to accomodate the tyres. Delivered in bare metal, F-101Bs were later painted gray to reduce corrosion. They were compatible with the Semi-Automatic Ground Environment (SAGE) system.

The Hughes MG-13 fire-control system was the 'brain' behind the Voodoo's mix of nuclear and non-nuclear air-to-air rockets but was something of a mismatch with the Voodoo airframe; it was considered inferior to the MA-1 system employed on the F-106. Armament was two GAR-8 (later AIM-4)

Falcon infrared air-to-air missiles and two nuclear-tipped MB-1 (later AIR-2A) Genie rockets. A plan to arm the aircraft with three Falcons and a tray of 2.75-inch folding fin aircraft rockets (FFAR) was never tested or adopted.

The Douglas MB-1 Genie (redesignated AIR-2A on 1 October 1962) was a 10 ft 4 in. (2.94 m) unguided projectile able to inflict punishment on bombers without a direct hit, since it carried a 1.5-kiloton atomic warhead. Genie was powered by a 36,000-lb (16,600-kg) thrust Thikiol solid rocket motor, weighed 822 lb (373 kg) at launch, and could fly at Mach 3.0 to hit bombers 5 to 6.2 miles (8 to 10 km) away. On 19 July 1957, the first live Genie was fired from an F-89J Scorpion at 15,000 ft (4572 m) over Yucca Flat, Nevada, the atomic warhead detonated

*NF-101B Voodoo (56-0232), the first two-seat interceptor, outside the St Louis plant before its 27 March 1957 first flight. Note non-standard wingtip fairings for test cameras. The F-101B test programme consumed two years and encountered setbacks typical of any such effort, but provided Air Defense Command with a thoroughly evaluated, combat-ready warplane capable of intercepting Soviet bombers at stand-off distance from their targets*

OVERLEAF
*Category II test flight at Edwards AFB. Test pilot Capt Donald M Sorlie (left) and engineer Kenneth C Carter in F-101B Voodoo (56-0236) in late 1958. A painter has inscribed the fact that the F-101B has made, or is making, its 100th flight while a graffiti artist has added the comment, 'No squawks'—[complaints]*
*(both MDC)*

TOP LEFT
The first Voodoo interceptor, NF-101B ( 56-0232) on its
27 March 1957 first flight with Robert C Little up front,
nobody in back
(MDC)

LEFT
The tiny '5-B' appearing on the tail of this Voodoo at
Edwards AFB, California, identifies it as the fifth F-101B
interceptor built. This airframe is understood to have been
used for stores carriage trials with the AIR-2A Genie
rocket, although it did not carry the full radar or fire-
control system of production machines
(via Marty J Isham)

William S Ross (left), McDonnell test pilot and Edward
M (Bud) Flesh (right), designer of the Voodoo, aboard an
F-101B interceptor at St Louis in December 1958. Ross
was later a test pilot on the F-4 Phantom and is now
McDonnell's vice president in charge of the F-15 Eagle
programme
(MDC)

for this test by ground control. Aboard the F-101B Voodoo, the overtaxed MG-13 fire-control system operated by the RO (radar observer) tracked the target, assigned the missile, commanded the pilot to arm the warhead, fired the missile (without a hand on any trigger), pulled the interceptor into a tight turn to escape the explosion, and finally triggered the warhead at the correct moment. Training version of the Genie was known as the MB-1-T, later ATR-2A.

The Hughes Falcon, first given the fighter designation XF-98, later GAR-8, later AIM-4 was widely employed in both infrared (IR) and semi-active radar homing (SARH) variants. 6 ft 5.8 in. (1.97 m) long, weighing 110 lb (50 kg) at launch, the Falcon had a range of about 6 miles (9.7 km). Never fired in anger by an F-101B, the Falcon was unsuccessful in its never-intended dogfight role in Vietnam where one pilot called it 'an inept, overly complicated, ugly piece of junk that did not work.' Against bombers, it *would* have worked.

From the second two-seater (56-233), all F-101Bs were strengthened for higher Gs. At Edwards AFB, Category I tests explored the general flying capabilities of the airplane. In Category II tests, ARDC tested the plane and its systems. Category III tests were a realistic evaluation by the using command, ADC.

From February 1957, Kenneth C Carter was a civilian test engineer for the Category II tests at Edwards. 'We experienced a number of trying incidents in about 60 hours of flight time with the F-101B [actually 64 flights covering 67 hours]. Our flight testing included maximum power climb, acceleration to maximum speed, speed-power tests, takeoffs and landings.' Major Walter F Daniel was project pilot for the F-101B 'Cat II' evaluations. The F-101B was powered by two 10,700-lb (4535-kg) thrust Pratt & Whitney J57-P-53 turbojets.

Ken Carter's first flight in the F-101B occurred in June 1958, one of 19 flights to assess performance, stability, and control. Pilot was Captain Donald M Sorlie, another future wearer of general's stars. Carter found the experience of the afterburner takeoff, rocket-like climbout, and view from 40,000 ft (12,192 m) to be truly unforgettable.

Evaluation of the interceptor became a dragged-out process though it eventually produced a superb, combat ready aircraft for ADC. Predictable difficulties were encountered with pitch-up, engine compressor stalls, and engine fuel control. Ken Carter made seven or eight test flights in the back seat of the F-101B serene in the knowledge that if anything went wrong, he could eject. Imagine, then, how Carter felt when Edwards Test Ops received a 'Red-X' safety-of-flight order grounding all F-101Bs for modification to the canopy opening cylinder. Rocket sled tests, conducted by McDonnell's E F Peters, had disintegrated two parachute dummies and torn up part of the track road bed. A high-speed camera film looking down the track is described by Peters as 'a

horror movie!' Carter was informed that sled tests showed that when the canopy was jettisoned, the canopy opening cylinder swung rearward, striking the occupant in the rear seat! An easy fix was found, and ADC legend holds that no back-seat radar observer (RO) was ever killed in a Voodoo ejection, even in instances where the front-seat pilot perished.

## Into Service

The 60th Fighter-Interceptor Squadron (FIS) at Otis AFB, Mass, was chosen to conduct the 'Cat III' suitability tests on the F-101B. The aircraft would be evaluated in an operational setting while beginning service. The first machine was delivered to Otis on 5 January 1959. During the test period, both SAGE and manual modes of intercept control were evaluated, the 60th being one of the squadrons which helped to develop the SAGE system under Project Grayfish.

In the 'Cat III' flying, targets were engaged at various distances, speeds and altitudes, these being aircraft types which ranged from T-33s to B-47s to a sole Bristol Britannia! The Category III tests encompassed numerous special projects including head-on geometries against the supersonic B-58 Hustler. 1st Lt Walter B Pearson was one of the first ROs in the 60th FIS to make the transition from F-94C Starfire to F-101B and remembers operational 'Red' (5 minute with conventional armament) and 'White' (nuclear) alerts. The 60th participated in the Cuban Missile Crisis and Pearson recalls that theirs was the fighter squadron closest to the Kennedy complex at Hyannisport. President Kennedy landed in Air Force One at Otis during his visits there, and the 60th stood honour guard for him.

## Into Service

In June 1959, F-101B Voodoo operations commenced with the 84th (Hamilton AFB, Calif), 98th (Dover AFB, Delaware) and 322nd (Kingsley Field, Oregon) squadrons. At the end of the year, these ADC units were joined by the 2nd (Suffolk County, NY), 13th (Glasgow AFB, Montana), 49th (Griffiss AFB, NY), 62nd (K I Sawyer AFB, Michigan) and 75th (Dow AFB, Maine) squadrons. A third stage of readiness was reached six months later in June 1960 when the F-101B Voodoo attained initial operating capability with the 15th (Davis-Monthan AFB, Ariz), 18th (Grand Forks AFB, ND), 29th (Malmstrom AFB, Montana), 87th (Lockbourne AFB, Ohio), 437th (Oxnard AFB, Calif), 444th (Charleston AFB, SC) and 445th (Wurtsmith AFB, Michigan). Finally, the 83rd FIS became operational with the interceptor Voodoo in August 1960. In twenty months, seventeen squadrons had begun F-101B operations and by June of 1960 the Voodoo had become the most numerous aircraft in ADC inventory, as it would remain for four years. A plan to

TOP
*F-101B (58-0320) of the 29th FIS based at Malmstrom
AFB, Montana, 4 March 1967*
*(A Swanberg via Norman Taylor)*

*F-101B (58-0259) of the 98th FIS based at Suffolk
County AFB, LI., NY. IR (infrared) seeker, just forward
of windshield, was a retrofit)*
*(B Esposito via Norman Taylor)*

station the 449th FIS at Ladd AFB, Alaska, did not reach fruition, however, even though incursions by Soviet aircraft in the Bering Sea were a continuing threat.

With a special nod of thanks to Walt Pearson and Jan Towery, an attempt will now be made to describe a typical F-101B mission.

## Flying the F-101B

Two F-101B Voodoos, each loaded with two 450 US-gal external fuel tanks, are towed from the 60th FIS flight line at Otis AFB, Mass, to the alert hangar area. Each aircraft is given final maintenance inspection and loaded with two AIM-4C Falcons. The two-man crews of RED 1 and RED 2 are notified by Maintenance that the airplanes are ready to be preflighted. Upon completion of a preflight check, the crews return to the ready room and settle-in for their 24-hour alert period. RED 1 and RED 2 are now on five-minute alert status. This fact is put into the SAGE computer, in a protected blockhouse which may be hundreds of miles away from the various fighter-interceptor squadrons that comprise a five-minute alert force.

At midnight, a blip appears on the SAGE surveillance radar screen. It is declared an unknown. The SAGE computer, using target position input information from various radars throughout the air defence early warning system, quickly computes the logical scramble force as being the 60th FIS at Otis AFB on Cape Cod since the 60th can make a minimum-time intercept. The computer automatically sounds the scramble horn at the 60th alert hangar. The aircrews and maintenance personnel, resting fully clothed in their bunks, are jarred from their semi-sleep state by the deafening blast of the scramble horn just outside the window of the crew quarters. As they scramble for the aircraft, each aircrew member pauses briefly at the foot of his cockpit ladder to don his cold-water survival suit, known in ADC as the 'Poopy Suit.'

As the pilot of each aircraft starts engines, the RO calls the tower for scramble instructions.

'Uh, Roger, RED 1. Callsigns X-RAY KILO zero-one and zero-two. Buster angels three-zero. Heading zero-niner-zero after Otis scramble cor-

TOP LEFT
*F-101B (57-0443) of the 437th FIS on a visit to Van Nuys, California, on 3 July 1966. This airplane later went to the CAF as 101064*
*(S Kraus via Norman Taylor)*

*F-101B (57-0322) of the 444th FIS based at Charleston AFB, SC, armed with the dummy ATR-2A version of the AIR-2A Genie nuclear rocket. Pictured on 28 December 1964 with F-106 in background*
*(Norman Taylor)*

ridor. Contact Otis departure control on three-zero-two-point-seven when airborne. Cleared to taxi.'

While taxying, the RO calls off the taxi checklist to the pilot and sets his datalink set to his callsign suffix number. This establishes a link between the SAGE computer and the aircraft. 'Otis tower, X-RAY KILO zero-one flight number one for the active.'

'Roger, zero-one. You are cleared for immediate takeoff. Contact departure when airborne.'

'Roger, Otis.' After running up both engines, 01 and 02 are ready to roll. Each pilot brings his engines to full throttle and the lead gives his wingman the visual signal for brake release. The afterburners are lit almost immediately after the start of the takeoff roll. The landing gear is retracted immediately after the aircraft are airborne to prevent the Voodoo's forward-retracting nose gear from becoming trapped, an embarrassing event that almost every Voodoo pilot has experienced in cold climates. The flaps are retracted and the afterburners terminated soon thereafter. The elapsed time from scramble horn to wheels-up is four minutes and thirty seconds. The five-minute response time has again been satisfied.

'Zero-two, let's go to departure frequency.' 02 acknowledges and both ROs tune in the departure frequency.

'Otis departure, X-RAY KILO 01 established in the corridor climbing.'

'Roger, zero-one. Continue corridor departure. Call over P-town. [Provincetown, at the tip of Cape Cod].'

'Roger, Otis.' As the climb continues at military power ('buster'), the RO is finishing the climb checklist call-out to the pilot and adjusting the MG-13 fire-control radar for best performance and display. 01 flight begins to have fleeting thoughts about the unknown out there over the North Atlantic. What is it? A computer-generated target, a ghost blip that sometimes plagues the SAGE computer? An airliner? A SAC B-47 or B-52? A Navy P2V at low altitude in the soup again? Or is the first detectable target entering the system as a part of a Soviet attack?

'Otis departure, X-RAY zero-one flight over P-town at seventeen thousand feet [5181 m], climbing.'

'Roger, zero-one. Turn right to zero-niner-zero and continue climb to flight level three-zero-zero. Contact Greyfish control on three-twenty-seven-point-five. Good luck, sir.'

The flight leader informs Greyfish Control that his flight is 'passing angels two-five to three-zero [25,000 to 30,000 ft, or 7620 to 9144 m]. Heading is zero-niner-zero buster.'

'Roger, zero-one flight,' the ground controller responds. 'We need altitude, heading, aircraft type, speed and tail numbers on this guy. Follow dolly.' Zero-one flight knows from the last instruction to follow the commands and information provided on the datalink cockpit displays and to observe radio silence until the identification intercept is complete.

The command altitude indicators in both Voodoos indicate 35,000 ft (10,668 m) and the command Mach meter 0.9 Mach. The datalink steering dot on the pilot's radar display and the target marker circle on the RO's scope indicate dead-ahead. The climb is continued to 35,000 ft (10,668 m) and both aircraft level off and set their speeds at the command Mach number. The RO's target marker circle indicates that the target is dead-ahead at 45 miles (73 km). 02 breaks away from 01 when the target marker indicates 30 miles (48 km) and the pilot's steering dot shows a sudden deflection. (In the ADC tactics scenario, one of the RED aircraft makes the identification pass while the other stands off for a firing pass if needed. In this case, the SAGE computer is transmitting information to 02 that will result in his being positioned at the stand-off location. The pilot-RO cockpit exchange continues as 01 presses in for the identification pass . . .

'Target dead-ahead at 25 miles [40 km]. Confirm viz-ident mode selected.' The pilot checks his armament control panel and confirms that the mode selector switch is positioned for an identification pass. Suddenly, the target marker circle deflects to the left and centres at a range of 20 miles (30 km). The RO continues to search the area of the target marker circle for his assigned target.

'Contact forty-five degrees port at twenty miles [30 km]. Port. Disregard dolly.' The SAGE computer has fulfilled its function of getting the interceptor grossly positioned in the target area. The intercept control is now in the hands of the RO and he instructs the pilot to disregard the datalink indications. The RO quickly analyses the target blip drift characteristics on his screen and determines that the gross geometry is one of reciprocal headings with lateral displacement; his first action is to instruct the pilot to turn left using twenty degrees of bank ('port' command). He continues to watch the drift characteristics of the blip while reporting range and azimuth to the pilot. The pilot continuously scans for a visual sighting on the target. Luckily, tonight is a clear night. However, with weather present or the target 'blacked out' (navigation lights turned off), the pilot must depend on the RO to keep him informed of target position and to accurately and safely bring the aircraft into final visual identification position.

In the port turn, the RO notices that the blip is sliding out in azimuth on his scope, so he instructs the pilot to increase his rate-of-turn to maximum. 'Port hard as possible.' The pilot immediately increases his speed and bank angle. The RO notices that the drift has stopped and he watches his scope for the first indicating that the blip is starting to drift toward the centre of his scope. Here, safety is of paramount importance because should the target hold at one azimuth on the RO's B-scan type display, a collision is certain if something in the geometry is not changed. 'Target forty-five degrees port at fifteen miles [24 km], overtake seven hundred-eighty knots [1090 km/h].' At 14 miles (23 km), the blip starts to move rapidly across the scope toward zero-azimuth. 'Ease off. Hold.' The RO has the drift he is looking for and he now begins to 'fine-tune' the geometry so that the target is placed on the nose at ten miles with ninety degrees of heading difference, commonly called the 'ninety-ten' tactic in ADC. The pilot increases or decreases his bank angle and holds as the RO instructs. 'Target dead-ahead at ten miles [16 km].' The RO begins to look for the blip to start drifting to port as the target passes the nose. He sees the drift starting to develop and instructs the pilot, 'Port.' The pilot establishes twenty degrees of bank. This turn rate stops the drift and the target is staying dead-ahead in azimuth. The Voodoo is in a turn that will eventually result in a roll-out dead-astern of the target at about five miles (8 km). The range rate meter starts to show a fall-off in overtake. The RO continues to 'fine-tune' the geometry through instructions to the pilot to assure that an excessively long roll-out range does not occur that will result in more time for the intercept; likewise, he must assure that a dangerous situation is not set up by rolling out too close to the target. 'Target dead-ahead at five miles [8 km]. Overtake fifty knots [86 km/h].' An optimum roll-out has resulted.

'Re-check viz-ident and armament safety switch off and safety-wired.' 'Roger,' the pilot confirms.

'Fly the dot,' instructs the RO. He has locked his radar on to the target and released the intercept control back to the pilot. He continues to give the pilot geometry and overtake information as the range is closed toward the final intercept point. The pilot flies the MG-13 FCS computer-generated steering dot; it will take the aircraft to a position that is two hundred feet (61 m) right of the target and two hundred yards (190 m) slant range, at which point he will get a pull-out signal that indicates that the final position has been reached. From that point, the pilot controls the intercept to a position that is optimum for identification purposes.

'Target three degrees port, seven hundred yards [650 m]. Overtake is holding at fifty knots [86 km/h].' 'Roger. Tally-ho,' the pilot replies as he confirms a visual on the target.

'Target five degrees port, two hundred yards [190 m]. Overtake ten knots [19 km/h].'

'Roger. I have a pull-out signal. Stand by for ID light.'

'Roger. Ready with ID light. Overtake slightly positive. Good position.' The pilot adjusts the throttles so that he is at the same airspeed as the target.

'ID light on.' The RO switches on the 8-inch sealed beam light located on the fuselage near his cockpit. A commercial airliner is readily identified as window shades begin to open and passengers gawk out at the Voodoo stalking them in the night. The 8-inch light is powerful enough to upset the passengers considerably.

As the pilot flies formation with the target, the RO calls in the required information to Ground Control Intercept (GCI) control. 'Grayfish, X-RAY KILO zero-one.'

'Roger, zero-one. Ready to copy.'

'Pan Am seven-o-seven [Boeing 707], angels three-five [35,000 feet, or 10,668 m], heading two-six-five degrees at three-hundred-and-ten knots [520 km/h] indicated. Tail number six-zero-two-seven-six.'

'Roger, zero-one. Clear target and follow dolly. Zero-two will be joining up in approximately five minutes.'

The SAGE computer transits datalink information to both aircraft that will result in their rejoining and returning to base. They are handed off to Otis approach control and brought in for a GCA and landing. On the ground, both aircraft are refuelled and pre-flighted and the Air Division headquarters is notified that RED 01 and RED 02 are turned around and once again on five-minute alert status.

Fortunately, no target ever turned out to be a Russian bomber heralding the onset of a world war. But Voodoo pilots, ROs, and maintenance men always knew it was possible.

## Undeserved Reputation

Given its size and complexity, the F-101B Voodoo (and the 'F-101B dual control equipment airplanes' which were known at various times as F-101F, TF-101B, TF-101F, etc) was a remarkably safe aircraft. Radar observers are a cynical breed, however. One backseater composed a musical ode to the Voodoo entitled 'McDonnell's Flying Outhouse.'

Another RO was Roger K (Roby) Roberson. In June 1960, Roberson flew his last training mission in the F-89J Scorpion at James Connally AFB, Texas, where radar observers were trained, and was graduated second in his class. Given his second choice of assignment, Roberson picked the 437th FIS at Oxnard AFB, California, which had become operational with the F-101B Voodoo three months earlier. To celebrate the anniversary of American independence, Roberson arrived at Oxnard on 4 July 1960 in a '55 Mercury with a pregnant wife and a beagle hound dog named Snooper. The squadron despatcher pointed out that it was a holiday and explained that everybody was at a picnic at the Officers Club. So Roberson and family, beagle

OVERLEAF
*Led by aircraft 57-420, three F-101B Voodoos of the 2nd FIS pass by the United Nations building in New York city in 1966. At this time, base commander at Suffolk County AFB, New York was Colonel Francis S Gabreski, the top living US air ace with 37 kills in World War 2 and 6½ MiG victories in Korea*
*(via Col Frank D Bingham)*

included, descended on the Club where Voodoo flier Gabby Haynes was grilling T-bone steaks. Ticket-seller at the squadron holiday dinner, the first officer in the 437th to introduce himself to the newcomer, was 1st Lt Robert D Russ. The future chief of Tactical Air Command had become one of the few Voodoo people to shift from the single-seaters at Bentwaters/Woodbridge to the interceptor variant.

Roberson recalls flying the Voodoo in William Tell shootout competitions, by now shifted to the ADC bastion at Tyndall AFB in the Florida panhandle. Squadron mate Richard E McCoy had flamed out a F-89J Scorpion two miles from the approach end of Tyndall's runway and more than a year later during the May 1961 William Tell Meet the Scorpion still protruded from the swamp on the Tyndall approach, glinting in the sun, a reminder.

## Flying the F-101B (II)

'At William Tell, we competed with F-102 and F-106 squadrons. Squadrons got 'points' for maintenance, 'in-commission' aircraft, launch rate, distance of pick-up and lock-on, rocket/missile reliability, and a 'kill factor.' The Voodoo squadrons racked up so many more points than F-102 and F-106 squadrons that ADC decided to rate Voodoo squadrons *only* against *each other* because we made the other aircraft types look bad.' Roberson goes on to give *his* version

of an intercept from the back seat:

'You're at 46,000 ft [14,020 m] and 1.3 Mach and you pick up a target 10 degrees to starboard, 30 miles [48 km] away. At 20 miles [32 km], the RO must get a good radar lock-on and tell the pilot to "steer the dot." Now the pilot couples the "attack display" to the autopilot and the Voodoo flies itself. It snaps up above 50,000 ft [15,240 m] and [automatically] fires, hands off.

'The ride you get after the autopilot takes over is called the "Voodoo dance." The autopilot trying to steer the dot bumps you around the canopy like spam in a can.'

ROs have so many Voodoo stories, some unbelievable, some unprintable, that they would require a separate volume. One of Roberson's tales, using first-names only:

'John was in my RI [radar intercept] class and took an assignment to [the 98th FIS at] Dover AFB, Delaware. They did a lot of their high-altitude intercepts way out over the water. One day John and his pilot "pitched up" and ejected at 15,000 ft [4572 m]. John looked up and saw a good canopy and when he looked down all he could see was water. He dearly loved Chesterfield cigarettes and thought, "Oh, shoot! I'm going to get 'em all wet!" So he got one out, lit it up, and smoked it all the way to splashdown. He got in his rubber raft and after awhile came a rescue helicopter and picked him and his pilot up.

*Major Del Jacobs (later a major general) did much of the flying work on the ATAR (air-to-air recognition) system denoted by the unusual bulge beneath the nose of F-101B Voodoo (57-0272) seen at Tyndall AFB, Florida, on 22 September 1972. Aircraft belongs to the Air Defense Weapons Center (ADWC)*
(Norman Taylor)

LEFT
*Roger Roberson, one of the radar observers (ROs) of the F-101B era, arrived at Oxnard AFB on Independence Day 1960 with a '55 Mercury, a pregnant wife, and a beagle dog named Snooper. Roberson went on to fly the F-101B in two squadrons with the Air Defense Command*
(Roberson)

OVERLEAF
*F-101F Voodoo (58-317) dual-control equipment aircraft with the experimental ATAR system (fairing beneath nose) at Tyndall on 25 September 1978. ATAR was a kind of predecessor of the TISEO (target identification system, electro-optical) introduced by McDonnell on late-model F-4E Phantoms*
(Norman Taylor)

The chopper's loadmaster [probably actually a para-jumper, or PJ] helped them on board but told them, "Don't take off your water wings. We don't have enough gas to get back to land." So the chopper pilot found a submarine on the surface and ditched beside it. The F-101B crew swam across to the sub, were fed steaks for supper, and had a nice safe ride back to shore.' As evidence that not *all* of Roberson's stories involve T-bone steaks, he also says, 'We performed test intercepts which proved that the Voodoo had a 2 to 1 probability of killing a U-2 at the altitude Francis

Gary Powers was shot down over Russia. On missions against U-2s, I've been upside down at 55,000 feet [16,764 m] and seen 1,025 knots [1400 km/h] TAS [true indicated airspeed] during recovery.' In fact, Powers' actual altitude is a matter of historical dispute. Roberson made his final flight in the Voodoo with newly-promoted Captain Robert D Russ on 13 February 1962.

Another well-known F-101B Voodoo crewman, a pilot this time, was Major Cecil G Foster of the 28th FIS at Malmstrom AFB, Montana, who'd become an

*Seen at Eglin AFB, Florida, in May 1969 in this unusual
view supplied by air defence expert Marty J Isham, NF-
101B Voodoo 57-0409 had a unique, one-of-a-kind nose
configuration. Aircraft was used to test systems for surface-
to-air drones employed as targets at the Air Defense
Weapons Center at nearby Tyndall AFB, Florida*
( Jack D Morris)

ace in Korea by downing five MiG-15s. As operations officer of a Voodoo squadron, Foster was known for working extra hours, placing heavy demands to get his crews combat-ready, and keeping a quart of Rolaids on his desk. An RO who flew with Foster in an F-101B Voodoo (56-0294) on 27 July 1964 bestows upon him the highest accolade. 'The guy was a vicious killer of the enemy's airplanes. Where the book called for one firing pass and breakaway, Cecil would fire primary, press on in, reselect secondary armament, fire, and press on in for a "ram". We ran three intercepts one day and came back credited with five [simulated] kills. Cecil was a great leader and a great fighter pilot. And when things went wrong, he would chug-a-lug two or three Rolaids.'

The F-101B was also known to McAir (the term which eventually replaced MAC to refer to the McDonnell Aircraft Company) as the Model 36 AT, and to the US Air Force as Weapon System 217A. An official history states the radar observer's cockpit had been badly designed, although no RO contacted during the research for this volume said so. The drawbacks of the MG-13 fire-control system have been noted. Although support of the F-101B had initially been handicapped by shortages of parts, it improved by mid-1960 when supply and maintenance problems were well under control. In December 1960, nine of ADC's 17 squadrons were rated C-1—the highest degree of combat readiness—and seven were C-2. Only one squadron was considered deficient and this was due to a temporary shortage of qualified personnel. On average, 70 per cent of the 371 F-101B airframes then assigned to the combat forces were operationally ready. The numbers experts determined that the flyaway cost for an F-101B/F was $1,754,066 for the airframe, $1,105,034 for engines (when installed), $332,376 for electronics, and $262,885 for armament. It was recorded that average cost per flying hour was $1,004 and that average maintenance cost per flying hour was $501. The modifications to support the MB-1 (AIR-2A) Genie missile were authorized in July 1961, after all Voodoo airframes had been delivered.

## Mechanic's Eye View

The men who 'keep 'em flying' are, if anything, more important than the colourful figures who sit in the cockpits. Just as the Voodoo was never easy to fly, it was never easy to fix. But crewchiefs loved the airplane with a passion. Norman Stutts, who crewed two F-101B Voodoos (58-0313; 58-0339) with the 18th FIS in the very far north at Grand Forks AFB, North Dakota, in 1966–70 has no RO-style bar-room stories; true eloquence is vested in crewchief Stutts. 'The fact that the Voodoo served our country so well for over 30 years is testimony to the quality of the aircraft and to the maintenance [people] who kept it in service.' Adds Stutts:

'I spent many evenings on the flight line in zero (or below) weather on a maintenance stand fifteen feet [4.57 m] in the air removing a hundred brass screws (many will round out) to open a panel accessing a leaking pitch control servo. I have lain on my back or sat doubled-up in the intakes removing the "dog pecker," as we called the engine accessory section cover—aptly named for its shape—and either resealing or replacing the air reservoirs for the restart system. Also accessed from the intake and in the side of the fuselage behind the boundary layer duct is the air-oil cooler. After replacing one of these, one must spend the next couple of hours bathing the aircraft inside and out. By the time the job is completed, the crewchief is ready for some serious laundering himself.

'Ailerons and flap actuators required a good deal of attention also. Lest I be accused of being prejudiced against this aircraft, let me tell you that such is not the case. *Most* fighter aircraft tend toward hydraulic leaks in sub-zero weather. In warmer climates, the F-101B was not so troublesome.' Stutts adds that of the fighters he crewed in the Air Force (F-101B, T-33A, F-106A and A-7D), the Voodoo was the most gratifying. 'Daily exposure to the Voodoo for $3\frac{1}{2}$ years did not keep me from pausing to appreciate the airplane each time the brakes were released, the afterburners were lit, and the F-101B sought its element.'

And from the front seat? Most pilots radiate the same enthusiasm as their RO back-seaters. A few qualify their remarks. Colonel Jack Broughton, who did not spend much time in the airplane, says, 'The F-101B was not a difficult aircraft to fly but it always reminded me of a railroad train. Keep it on the tracks and it would probably do what it was supposed to do. It was not an aircraft that I ever became attached to and I never felt that the 101 and I were in it together. It was more like it would put up with me if I would put up with it and treat it with attention without affection.'

## Flying at Tyndall

The 4570th Test Squadron was the operational suitability test unit for ADC, which changed its name from Air to Aerospace Defense Command in the early 1970s. Pilots and ROs assigned to the 4750th were hand-picked at command level and selection was based on demonstrated expertise in the aircraft and experience. RO Walter B Pearson moved to Tyndall to participate in hundreds of projects related to he F-101B combat capability. One of these was the evaluation of the F-101B Block II IIP (interceptor improvement program) system. Another was the evaluation of a supersonic tow target system on the F-101B which was capable of stringing tow targets for missile exercises out to 49,000 feet (14,935 m) at a cable payout rate of 5,000 feet (1524 m) per minute. Yet another 4750th project, with Pearson on the scene, was the firing of over 100 missiles and rockets

from the F-101B against a myriad of targets, including the BQM-34/A Firebee drone, Quail, Hound Dog, BOMARC, and various tow targets. This was fascinating stuff, held at the same place as the regular William Tell meets, and when Pearson left the Air Force as a major in June 1969 with 2,500 flight hours in the F-101B he was the second most experienced RO in the service.

*F-101B tail markings of the 59th FIS: this unit was deactivated in 1970 and their airplanes passed to the 166th FIS, Washington ANG. 57-0278 pictured at Spokane, Washington, in May 1970 shortly after the handover (Norman Taylor)*

## Supersonic Tow System

The RMU-8A/TDU-9B supersonic tow system employed by the Voodoo, commonly known as 'Super Tow,' underwent Category I and II tests at Eglin AFB, Florida. The final part of Category II and all of Category III (user) tests were conducted by the 4750th at Tyndall, which is not far from Eglin and faces the Gulf of Mexico.

The Voodoo was modified with a centreline store structure just aft of the armament rotary door in order to provide hard points for mounting the RMU-8A tow reel. The RMU-8A, commonly referred to as the Rummy 8, weighed 825 lb (374 kg) and could carry up to 40,000 feet (12 192 m) of tow line. The reel was capable of reeling-out and retrieving tow targets in the 200-lb (90-kg) class at an average rate of 5,000 feet (1524 m) per minute. Reel controls were mounted in the RO's cockpit.

Three tow lines were used operationally at Tyndall—the 49,000-ft (14,935-m) THU-6A, the 27,000-ft (8229-m) THU-7A, and the 15,000-ft (4572-m) THU-8A.

The Hayes TDU-9B tow target was the first centre-of-gravity tow target design in the world. The target underwent many modifications during development. These evolved mainly as a result of an improving missile-scoring technology. The final configuration approached a length of seven feet (2.13 m), was nine inches (0.25 m) in diameter, and weighed slightly over 200 lb (90 kg). The target payload consisted of BIDOPS (By Doppler system) scoring for missiles, MATTS (Multiple Airborne Target Tracking System) scoring for ATR-2A Genie training rockets, active TWT augmentation for target radar cross section enhancement at X- and L-band frequencies, and four TAU-56B Infrared Augmentor Flares for IR missile guidance. The target was capable of supersonic flight and derived its power from a forward mounted air-driven generator. Sperry manufactured the second production run TDU-9B's and the target underwent numerous changes.

*Walt Pearson at the controls of Tyndall-based F-101B Voodoo (58-0277) carrying the RMU-8A ('Rummy 8')/TDU-9B supersonic target towing system. Tests on this supersonic target-tow were carried out by the 4750th Test Squadron at Tyndall*
*(Walter B Pearson)*

The last and most successful tow target developed for the F-101B/RMU-8A system was the Hayes TDU-25/B. This target was characterized by a continuous burning infrared source that used propane as the fuel and the most noise-free target environment ever provided for the Doppler family of scoring systems. Thousands were manufactured for support of the ADC low altitude Weapons System Evaluation Program (WSEP) and TAC Southeast Asia aircrew qualification firings (F-4/RMU-8A tow system). Other targets included the Sperry Improved TDU-9/B ('El Bandito') and Hayes TDU-22A/B.

First operational use of the Voodoo's Rummy 8/TDU-9B system was in support of the 1965 William Tell weapons competition. The system presentation was a 380 KIAS (knots, indicated air speed, or 535 km/h) at low level (500 ft/152 m) with the THU-8A tow line (15,000 ft/4572 m). Attack geometry/weapon was stern/infrared for the F-101B and F-106. Over 80 'Super Tow' sorties were flown by Tyndall crews in a five-day period. 'Super Tow' Voodoos were situated so as to keep a target on station almost continuously. On one firing pass, an F-106 passed inside the safe cable range limit and launched an AIM-4B Falcon infrared missile. The missile hit the tow line approximately 50 feet (15.2 m) aft of the

towing Voodoo's tailpipe, deflected off, and hit the
wingtip of the wingman. It deflected off again and
struck the bottom of the nose radome of the towing
Voodoo. Fortunately, there was no major damage to
the aircraft and nobody was hurt. The tow-target
capability remained an important part of the F-101B
Voodoo's story throughout its service with ADC.

Production of the Voodoo interceptor had ended
on 24 March 1961 when the 479th example was
delivered. The final 93 interceptor Voodoos were
completed to a slightly different standard and for a
brief period were identified as F-101Fs, this batch
being the source of the first group of 66 airframes
assigned to Canada in 1961. A major update of the
fire-control system known by the code name Kitty
Car resulted in earlier interceptor Voodoos being
brought up to this standard and, thereafter, all
interceptors were identified as F-101Bs. To further
confuse matters, the F-101F designation was then
applied to dual-control interceptors, although, as has
been noted, McDonnell always called them, simply,
F-101B dual control equipment airplanes.

## Air National Guardsmen

Once called 'weekend warriors' but, in fact, among
the best-trained and best-motivated pilots in American uniform, Air National Guard (ANG) officers
began to receive the F-101B/F Voodoo interceptor in
November 1969. Altogether, seven ANG squadrons
operated the interceptor, and a handful of dual-
control equipment airplanes were also operated by
the additional ANG squadrons which flew recce
Voodoos. Like a fine wine which reaches perfection

*F-101B Voodoo (57-0760) of the Washington Air
National Guard had been reduced to no more than a
derelict fuselage hulk when seen at Hill AFB, Utah, in the
winter of 1978*
*(Steve Camara)*

only with the passage of time, the Voodoo was at its
very best during the 1969–1983 period of service with
the Guard. Typical of achievements during this
period was that of the 178th FIS/119th FIG in far-off
Fargo, North Dakota, which won the Hughes
Trophy for air defence in 1974, the first time a Guard
unit had done so.

Throughout most of the Voodoo's ANG service,
the 111th FIS/147th FIG at Ellington AFB, Texas,
was the RTU (replacement training unit) which
trained and upgraded F-101B/F crews. The group
also won the 1978 and 1980 William Tell competitions in the F-101B category. This was, in fact,
the final Air Guard unit to operate the F-101B/F, and
the final unit in any of the American forces to fly the
Voodoo. Colonel Robert J Blissard, group commander, was in attendance on 8 August 1983 when
Major Nelson D DeStaffany went aloft in an F-101F
Voodoo (57-0352) to deliver the airplane to a display
location in California—the final Voodoo flight in the
annals of American arms. ANG units which had
flown the Voodoo converted to the F-4C/D Phantom.
Although it never saw combat like its reconnaissance
cousin, the F-101B contributed meaningfully to the
defence of the North American continent, and the
final act in its drama was played out north of the
border, when Canada became the only significant
foreign user of the Voodoo.

# Chapter 7
# The Watch on the Canadian Frontier
## Flying the CF-101B Up North

Canadians have long been rightly proud of their aircraft industry. The pride was justified by the Avro CF-100 Canuck, the fondly-remembered Clunk of the 1950s, an interceptor which guarded North American airspace and fulfilled Canada's NATO commitment. Pride and promise were never more evident than in the supremely advanced Avro CF-105 Arrow.

Men will probably be saying for years of the CF-105 Arrow (as they say of the British TSR.2) that it would have been the greatest warplane of its era, if only it had been mass-produced when it could have been. Group Captain Ned Frith, who flew the TSR.2, points out that with its vacuum-tube technology and unproven ordnance capability, the TSR.2 might not have been any sort of success at all. The CF-105 Arrow development programme went much farther, but its greatness was never assured.

Indeed, as early as 1953, Canada's air staff chief, Air Marshal Ray Slemon, might have looked south of the border to meet Operational Requirement 1/1-63 for a supersonic, all-weather interceptor to eventually replace the Clunk. Even while metal was being cut on the CF-105 Arrow, Slemon despatched an evaluation team under Wing Commander Ray Foottit to look at US interceptor designs as possible alternates. Foottit's team went to St Louis in 1953, when McDonnell's F-101B Voodoo had yet to fly. Although new at the time and long-legged by any measure, the F-101B did not seem right for Canada's requirements and apparently did not interest Foottit very much. Ottawa's air staff went forward with the very large CF-105 Arrow—as author Bill Gunston has pointed out, it had an internal missile bay larger than the bomb bay of a B-29!—and Canadians expected to continue building their own fighters.

The first of five Arrow 1 aircraft flew on 25 March 1958, powered by twin 23,500-lb (10,659-kg) thrust Pratt & Whitney J75-P-3 turbojets, although the production Arrow 2 would have had indigenous 28,000-lb (12,700-kg) thrust afterburning Orenda PS-13 Iroquois powerplants. Like the Clunk before it, the Arrow would have carried pilot and radar navigator/observer. 77 ft 9¾ in. (23.72 m) in length with a high-mounted delta wing, the Arrow was a giant gleaming white machine, immaculate and magnificent. Few aircraft that 'might have been' have ever seemed to offer more, TRS.2 included. Both were doomed by policymakers who believed in the late 1950s that missiles would replace airplanes—and by cost. For the Arrow, the budget axe came smashing down on 20 February 1959, ending a truly ambitious project.

Canada had already turned south of its border to order the Boeing IM-99 (later CIM-10) BOMARC surface-to-air missile for air defence. But missiles didn't replace airplanes, and still haven't. It soon became clear that the much-loved but weary Clunk could not serve past 1961 and that a long-range interceptor was still needed, to operate in conjunction with the NORAD (North American Air Defense Command) SAGE system. Only a manned interceptor could catch intruding Soviet bombers far from their intended targets and only a manned interceptor could be recalled in the middle of a mission. With the Arrow project scrapped, 'they had to take what they could get,' as Gunston puts it.

TOP RIGHT
*Stepped-up in immaculate formation, CF-100s (Mk 4Bs) of No 428 Sqn, Royal Canadian Air Force, glisten above the clouds*
(Hugh Mackechnie, Avro Canada)

*Before the sensational CF-105 Arrow interceptor (right) was shot down by political flak, it was expected to replace the CF-100 'Clunk' in RCAF squadrons. The Service had to fall back on a design it had earlier rejected—the F-101 Voodoo*
(Hugh Mackechnie, Avro Canada)

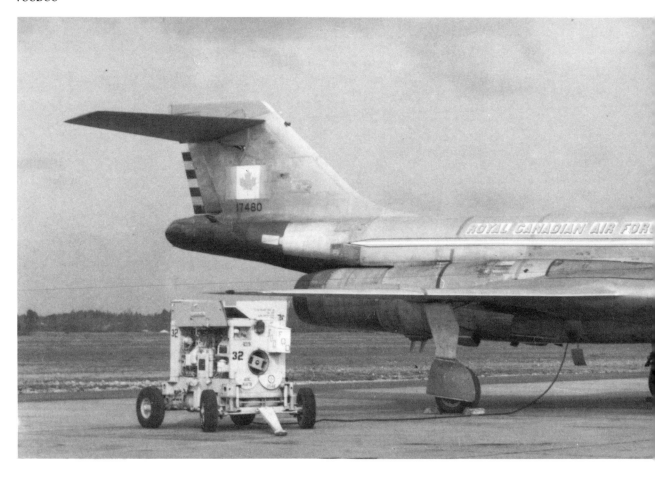

Under Operation Queens Row, the US supplied 66 Voodoos, including 56 F-101Bs and ten dual-control F-101Bs, the first of which were handed over at RCAF Upplands in April 1961. Historian Kevin Keaveney gives a different date, 13 November 1961, and notes that US Ambassador Livingston T Merchant was on the scene. The receipt for the Voodoos was reportedly signed by none other than Ray Foottit, who had been far from excited about the F-101 seven years earlier and could hardly have become more enthusiastic now that the Voodoos were older and, worse, second-hand. If there was an element of 'eating crow,' as one observer puts it, it must be remembered that the Voodoos were still very effective interceptors and, if never easy to fly, were well-liked by most crews who flew them. The aircraft were quickly designated CF-101B and CF-101F respectively. 'C' prefix or not, they had virtually no major components of Canadian manufacture.

It was in Canada that the Voodoo was used last. To put it another way, it is in Canadian service that the airplanes come closest to being 'contemporary' and there are still some very young men who flew the not-so-young CF-101 in Canadian skies. Their mission was, for most purposes, identical to that of the ADC fliers farther south.

The first 66 Voodoos delivered to Canada (for convenience, this narrative will speak of the 'first

*CF-101B (17480/59-0480) of No 414 Sqn, RCAF, based at CAFB Comox, Canada, prepares to depart after a visit to McChord AFB, Washington, on 27 April 1966. This airplane later crashed in Canada on 18 March 1968 (Norman Taylor)*

RIGHT
*A pair of CF-101Bs, serialled 17457 (nearest) and 17455, of No 414 Sqn, in RCAF markings, maintain close formation over one of Canada's many lakes in September 1963 (via S Isham)*

batch' and the 'second batch') had a nose inflight refuelling probe just forward of the pilot's windscreen, although air-refuelling was never used tactically in Canadian service.

## Equipment

CF-101B Voodoos were in most respects identical to US Air Force F-101B aircraft. By the early 1960s, several variants of the Falcon missile were in use. The AIM-4D was replaced in RCAF service by the AIM-42B variant, developed in 1963. Canada is understood to have acquired 200 AIM-4D and 400 AIM-26B missiles. In addition, CF-101B airplanes carried the AIR-2A Genie rocket projectile. Since the US by

official policy does not provide atomic warheads to other nations, even the friendliest (and also, as a matter of policy, does not comment on the subject), it must be assumed that Genies actually employed were for training purposes and may have been the ATR-2A variant. It can be speculated that some contingency arrangement must have existed to provide Canada with atomic warheads.

During test manoeuvres, CF-101B Voodoos also carried a McDonnell Simulator Rocket (MSR) RO-104/AJG on the port side of the lower fuselage, counter-balancing a Genie. A 'travel pod,' or baggage container, rather generous in size, could be fitted in the CF-101B forward nose when the aircraft was unarmed. Datalink antennas compatible with the SAGE system and identical to those employed by American Voodoos were also fitted, and the aircraft could carry two standard 450 US-gal belly tanks (together with the travel pod, if desired). Most F-101Bs were delivered with the all-important spot-light, for night operations, mounted just below the aft cockpit railing and used for visual identification of targets.

The 'second batch' of 66 Voodoos contained a retrofit also found on their American counterparts, namely a nose-mounted infrared sensor ball used for target detection. Cryogenic support gear for this system was mounted in the bay formerly occupied by the retractable inflight refuelling probe. Standard equipment on the CF-101B included AN/APX-72 transponder set, marker beacon, AN/ARC-34 UHF radio, ADF, AN/ARN-21 TACAN navigation radio, localizer, ILS, windshield defrost/defog, AN/AIC-10 intercom, AN/ARN-31 glide slope and localizer

*Bilingual Voodoo: CF-101B (17395) of No 416 Sqn, CAF, stands in wet weather in July 1960 (C Loring)*

TOP RIGHT
*CF-101B (101008) of No 416 Sqn, CAF, taxies out at Tyndall AFB, Florida, during the William-Tell Weapons Meet in September 1972 (Norman Taylor)*

receiver system, AN/ARN-32 marker beacon receiver, and an AN/APX-25 identification radar (IFF). It has been noted that the Webber ejection seat provided for pilot and RO did *not* have a zero-zero capability and was generally considered unsafe for bailout below an altitude of 900 feet (274 m). Once the Voodoo became rather long in the tooth in its final, northern climes, this *had* to be a morale factor.

The Canadian Voodoos went to the five RCAF squadrons listed in Appendix 8. Aircraft 59-0460 (17460) of No 416 Sqn at Chatham took Prime Minister Pierre Trudeau on an orientation flight in May 1968. When this airframe was later lost in a crash with No 410 Sqn at Cold Lake, it is almost certain that the by-then anachronistic ejection seat was a factor in the death of pilot and RO. This loss occurred on 20 November 1970, and one Canadian officer has opined that a zero-zero seat would have saved the crew. By then, virtually every other major fighter type in the world had an ejection seat designed to be functional at zero speed, zero altitude so that a crewman could escape from his aircraft, if necessary, even when parked on the ramp.

Of the 'first batch' delivered in 1961, 47 CF-101Bs (of 56) and nine CF-101Fs (of 10) survived. These 'first batch' airplanes went through a period of changes in their nation. The Canadian flag changed. The Royal Canadian Air Force was merged into the Canadian Armed Forces. And with renewed emphasis on the bilingual nature of Canadian society, both the English and French languages were employed on aircraft markings. By the time the 'second batch' of 66 Voodoos went to Canada (below), being distinguished externally primarily by the nose IR probe, Canadian Armed Forces (CAF) aircraft had attained a rather standardized and, it must be added, lacklustre set of markings. A few individual airframes were yet to be painted colourfully, but the standard Canadian paint scheme for the Voodoo was, as one officer put it, 'Blah.' The fuselage cheat line painted on every standard CF-101B with but one exception seems not to have been especially attractive for this type of aircraft.

In 1961, the 'second batch' of older but lower-hour Voodoos were exchanged for the first, the 66 machines again comprising 56 CF-101Bs and 10 CF-101F dual-control airplanes. The second batch transited through Winnipeg, where Bristol Aerospace Limited performed minor modifications. The new Voodoos were delivered to the CAF under Operation Peace Wings and represented an improvement in intercept capability: with the nose IR sensor, the RO could lock on a target and obtain direction and tracking, although not distance. Distance had to be estimated, based upon a reading from a heat-intensity indicator slaved to the IR sensor.

By the time this narrative was in preparation, only two Voodoos remained in service with No 414 Sqn located at CAF North Bay. CF-101F 56-0324 (CAF 101006, the 'second batch' airplanes having been assigned six-digit serials in accordance with current CAF practice) was the final survivor of the 'second batch' and was being employed in a training capacity, although it was thought that the airframe would be out of service before the end of 1986. This left only the EF-101B 58-0300 (CAF 101067) which was leased separately from the US Air Force, was *not* part of either 'batch,' and was therefore the 133rd and last Voodoo bailed to Canada. The EF-101B was also assigned to No 414 Sqn at CAF North Bay, apparently as the beneficiary of the training provided in the penultimate airframe, and was used for electronic counter-measures operations. This machine was painted in a sinister black scheme and had the only low-visibility national insignia applied to any Canadian Voodoo. In 1986, as evidence that very little had changed since the Voodoo design first began to take shape forty years earlier, the sole EF-101B suffered minor damage as a result of a landing gear failure!

## Voodoo Incident

Canada seems to have enjoyed a better safety record with the Voodoo than any other user. As noted, ten machines (out of 66) were lost in the 'first batch' over a full decade. 18 machines in the 'second batch' were lost in the final twelve years of operation—28 airframes lost in 22 years, in all.

The very last crash involving a Canadian Voodoo, or any Voodoo for that matter, occurred on 22 June

1984 when CF-101F 56-0328 (CAF 101007) of No 409 Sqn was lost near CFB (Canadian Forces Base) Comox, on the east coast of Vancouver island. The squadron was, in fact, scheduled to close down Voodoo operations a week later on 1 July 1984 and, as one observer puts it, 'Our final week was enlivened considerably by the timely ejections of Captains Tom Chester and Bernie Hughes from 007 as it was climbing out on an early morning mission.' While the official report on the incident was not available to the author, it was understood from talking with CAF officers that a blade from the 16th stage compressor of the J57 engine detached and sliced through a fuel tank with an immediate local explosion. The aircraft then went into an immediate flat spin. As a CF-101F, it had dual controls. It is understood that Hughes was flying from the back seat when the explosion occurred. Chester took control and noted a 0 (a zero) on the airspeed indicator! Hughes remembered seeing the same point on the horizon go by two or three times. The ejection seat had been improved considerably by the end of the Voodoo's career, but it *still* was not considered safe at low altitude and the pair wasted no time in pulling the handles to punch out.

A light aircraft pilot who witnessed the event reported that he saw the chutes open up scant seconds before 'Double Oh Seven' exploded and was engulfed in a fireball. The crew were lucky to land on nearby Texada Island with only minor injuries.

As has been noted with respect to Voodoo markings, the CAF, being a federal institution, is required by law to not merely accomodate but promote the French language in Canada. (Telephone receptionists at embassies abroad are required to greet any caller with, 'Canadian Embassy, *Bonjour*,' even though almost none would be able to continue the conversation in French if the caller wanted). All official CAF documents are published in both languages and this means that many routine working manuals and tech orders on Voodoo operations used up twice as much paper as might have been expected. There are people in the CAF who belong to French-language units who cannot speak English and who don't have to because the unit operates in French. This was changing, in the final days of the Voodoo's career, as progress was made towards bilingualism.

## The Making of a 'Nav'

Captain Mark Forseille typifies the highly-disciplined, thoroughly dedicated back-seater of the CF-101B Voodoo, in Canada called a navigator rather than an RO. Not every boy who likes aviation can actually end up as a crewman in the 'hot', powerful Voodoo, but Mark survived the rigours of training to become one of the few successful Voodoo

*Old Voodoo in new feathers: CAF CF-101B of No 409 Sqn, serial 17456, is ex-83rd FIS airplane 59-456. Photo taken in July 1969*
(no credit)

candidates at the end of the airplane's career in the 1980s 'I have flown in many aircraft, including the CF-5, CF-104, F-4, T-33 and the CF-18 as well as the Voodoo. [The Voodoo is] still my favourite. There is nothing to compare to the sound and feel of the 'hard' burners kicking in at low level, especially on takeoff on a cold day. It would rattle all of the windows on the base, pound on your chest and echo in your ears. The aircraft was less than perfect in the handling arena. It had a very good roll rate, but no nose authority. It couldn't turn a complete circle without crossing at least two provincial borders and it had a terrifying tendency to pitch-up at high angles of attack and low air speeds. But it sure could accelerate!'

Mark Forseille began his military career with 'boot camp' at CGB Chilliwack in the interior of British Columbia. This initial training lasted 13 weeks at which time Mark was classed as an officer cadet. Thereafter, Mark went to the CAF Air Navigation School at CFB Winnipeg, Manitoba, still as a cadet, where he spent almost a year (July 1979 to June 1980). At Winnipeg, this typical future CAF officer was instructed in the basics of air navigation and flew training missions in the C-130 Hercules. Upon graduation from 'Nav' school, Forseille and his classmates were given wings and commissions as second lieutenants.

The last stage of training was conducted at CFB Bagotville in Quebec, beginning in July 1980. There, Mark joined the 410th OTS (Operational Training Squadron) and began to learn the basics of being a fast-jet 'backseater.' It is perhaps worth mentioning that the 410th OTS still exists today, having moved to CFB Cold Lake, Alberta, where it trains pilots of the newer CF-18 fighter—which, incidentally, is not known as the Hornet in Canadian service because the name is not bilingual.

'The course in Bagotville was an adventure for me in many ways. The course material was challenging and the social life was incredible. The first few trips in the Voodoo, however, overshadowed everything else. It was an experience I'll always treasure. There were four navigators and four pilots on each course. At the end of the course, when the instructors thought that the pilots were safe fliers and the navigators were competent radar operators, there was an internal competition in the form of an air defence exercise. Various target aircraft were arranged and the students were paired up in teams. The competition was known locally as the Witch Hunt. At the end of the competition, there was a celebration and the traditional Witches Brew was served. This was an evil green concoction (designed and manufactured by the instructors; it was drunk only by the students). Modesty prevents me from saying who won the Witch Hunt. Let me just say it wasn't any of the other guys.' Between Hercules at Winnipeg and Voodoo at Bagotville, Mark's training had included flights in the Tutor and T-33 trainers.

After his February 1981 graduation from 'Bagtown,' our typical Voodoo navigator was posted to No 409 Sqn at CFB Comox. It was an assignment highly-desired by most English-speaking CAF officers. Because two of Mark's classmates were native Quebecois—one with the unlikely name of Pierre Trudeau—they preferred simply to move across the field at Bagotville to join No 425 'Alouette' Sqn.

From March 1981 to June 1984, most of Mark's flying was done over the Rocky Mountains. He notes that the scenery on a clear day was breathtaking. No 409 Sqn's commander was Lt Col Larry Lott, a much-respected and well-liked leader who maintained discipline and combat effectiveness without losing morale. 'Life on squadron generally consisted of holding "Q" (QRA or Quick Reaction Alert) or flying off the "line". We generally did a Q a week (two crews were on duty for 24 hours) until the squadron went to half strength in the summer of 1983 in preparation for conversion to the CF-18. During Mark's final year there, ending June 1984, crews averaged two Qs each week, sacrificing considerable free time to maintain a high state of alert.

The CF-101B navigator participated in many deployments and exercises, including Combat Pike, William Tell and Maple Flag. The last-named is a Canadian-sponsored tactical exercise which includes a wide variety of combat aircraft from the US, Canada, and NATO allies. No 409 Sqn also participated in public events, fielding an air show team every year. This team would travel to air shows in the US and Canada and perform precision formation flying. The navigators considered themselves to be more or less just 'along for the ride' on these occasions, but it was an enjoyable and interesting experience. Mark was on the air show team in 1982 with American exchange pilot Captain Bob Slack.

'It seemed that any time anything out of the ordinary happened, Bob Slack was my pilot. I was on two "live" scrambles out of the Q. Both times, Bob was driving. We had a small incident just after Christmas 1982. The main right landing gear on our jet [CF-101B 57-0432, CAF 101059] wouldn't lock in the down position. It collapsed on landing.'

Because the landing gear of the Voodoo has been the culprit in so many incidents, Captain Forseille was asked to elaborate on this one. 'The mission itself was routine and nothing was amiss until we joined the circuit and lowered the gear. Number Two was flying about one-half mile [804 m] behind. He reported that our right main gear flapped down and waggled instead of lowering slowly and locking as per normal. The green light did not illuminate to indicate a locked strut, so we knew that we had a problem. We went through the checklist and tried all the things we could, but to no avail. The mechanical locking mechanism was broken, so there was nothing that we could do, but of course we weren't sure about this at the time.

*CF-101B Voodoo (59-0453; CAF 17453) waits to acquire*
*storage number FF200 at the Military Aircraft Storage*
*and Disposition Center (MASDC), Davis-Monthan AFB,*
*Arizona, on 10 May 1971 following its return to the US*
*from Canada. This machine was later converted to*
*RF-101B standard and served with the Nevada Air*
*National Guard*
*(Douglas D Olson)*

'The only options were to punch out or to ride it in. We chose the latter, hoping for the best. The gear held up as we touched down, but began to fold under as we slowed through 120 knots [210 km/h].

'It finally collapsed and we skidded to the right and off the runway. We came to a rest finally and exited the aircraft with no injuries whatsoever . . .'

Since the Voodoo has ceased its role as an operational warplane, Mark Forseille has taken up a new posting with the CAF in Germany.

TOP LEFT
*Close-up of CF-101B (101057) of an unknown CAF unit participating in the William-Tell Weapons Meet at Tyndall AFB, Florida, 11 October 1980. Texas ANG Voodoos in background*
(Norman Taylor)

BOTTOM LEFT
*CF-101B Voodoo, serial 101046, of No 425 'Alouettes' Sqn, CAF, makes its way to the hammerhead at CFB Trenton in September 1981*
(Douglas R Tachauer)

BELOW
*CF-101B Voodoo, serial 101045, of No 416 'Lynx Squadron', CAF, parked at Trenton in September 1982*
(Philip A Tachauer)

## The Russian Bear

Because No 416 Sqn, the 'Black Lynx' squadron, operated from CFB Chatham, New Brunswick, on Canada's east coast, it was the only Canadian unit which regularly intercepted Soviet aircraft. The squadron's Voodoo pilots and navigators became accustomed, over the years, to escorting Soviet Tupolev Tu-95 *Bear* bombers en route from the USSR to Cuba.

In Operation Cold Shaft, which began 1 July 1982, the aforementioned practice of keeping half-strength units on longer periods of alert resulted in a number of intercepts by other squadrons. No 425 Sqn, or 'Alouette' squadron, maintained Voodoo detachments at various locations, including Loring AFB, Maine on US soil, and was charged with holding one-hour alerts as contrasted with the traditional 5-minute alerts. When scrambled, a pair of Voodoos was expected to be in the air and en route to Gander within one hour. At Gander, they would refuel and then go into anchor orbit offshore to be ready for the Russians. 425 thus had more than one opportunity to fly side-by-side with the Tupolev Tu-95, or *Bear-D*. On practice missions, Canadian Voodoo crews regularly rehearsed the intercept geometries which would enable them to intercept and engage newer, faster Soviet bombers as well as cruise missiles.

No 416 Sqn maintained the Cold Shaft alert commitment when it became the final operational

CF-101B Voodoo squadron in 1984. As late as October 1984, the squadron despatched four CF-101B Voodoos to Nellis AFB, Nevada, to 'bounce' the bombers taking part in the Strategic Air Command's Giant Voice bombing competition. In its final days, the squadron also fielded a pair of Voodoos, referred to as the 'Bobcats,' which participated in air shows throughout 1984, providing crowds with a fine exhibition of low-level manoeuvring and with the sudden bang of afterburners being cut in. The 'Bobcats' curtain call took place at the Shearwater International Air Show in September 1984, before a large crowd, where the CF-101B Voodoos shared the limelight with a performance by the A-4 Skyhawks of the US Navy's 'Blue Angels' aerobatic team.

The 'Bobcats' are among a number of CF-101B Voodoos still in storage in Canada.

## Colourful Voodoos

Whatever else may be said of the interceptor Voodoo, no one has seriously accused the aircraft of being especially colourful. The Canadian Armed Forces set forth to rectify this with five airframes that have been painted in unusually imaginative, eye-catching colour schemes. It began in 1977 when No 409 Sqn celebrated its 25th year of active service by painting a CF-101B Voodoo (57-0293, CAF 101012) as *Hawk One Canada*. The aircraft had an elaborate, blue-based paint scheme and a nighthawk with a beak. This machine eventually reverted to standard colours and, at the time, no one knew that several more brightly-hued Voodoos would follow in seven years' time.

To mark the 60th anniversary of Canadian military aviation, the squadron resurrected an almost identical paint scheme for another CF-101B (57-0429, CAF 101057). The second *Hawk One Canada* was almost indistinguishable from the first, although the nighthawk had a slightly different beak. Even the crew's baggage carrier (travel pod) was painted to conform with the overall colour scheme!

This time, however, there was competition. The 60th anniversary was also marked by No 416 Sqn at CFB Chatham which made innovative use of paint to create *Lynx Squadron Canada*, another CF-101B (57-0380, CAF 101043), which is illustrated in this volume. If an opinion may be dared, 'Lynx' is the best of the five special paint jobs affixed to Canada's Voodoos. The principal colours employed are black and white, with a grey lynx looking forward from a red field on the nose of the airplane.

To round out a trio of specially-marked machines for the 60th anniversary of military aviation in Canada, No 425 Sqn fielded *Lark One Canada*, as the name appears on one side of the fuselage or, in French on the other side, *Alouette Un Canada*, this being a CF-101B Voodoo (57-0298, CAF 101014) with blue nose and a red lark with a white head occupying the entire rear fuselage.

Finally, a paint scheme which might be described more as sinister than colourful appears on the 133rd and last Voodoo in Canadian service, which is also the final Voodoo to fly operationally anywhere in the world, the sole EF-101B.

# The EF-101B

*In approach configuration, Lynx Squadron Canada's spectacular CF-101B (101043) leads its No 416 Sqn CF-101B stablemate (101065) near the end of a sortie on 27 September 1984*
(Robbie Shaw)

*CF-101B Voodoo 101065 (USAF 57-444) c/n 622 wears the name* Lynx Squadron *beneath that unit's badge on its vertical tail on 27 September 1984. The squadron, one of those which operated the Voodoo toward the end of its service career, flew from CFB Chatham, New Brunswick*
(Robbie Shaw)

BELOW
*Taxying in rare sunlight is CF-101B serial 101060 (former USAF 57-433) c/n 757, showing markings typical of the Voodoo at the end of its service life in Canada. No 409 Sqn, the 'Nighthawks,' received the CF-101B at Namao in February 1962 and moved to CFB Comox in March 1962. The squadron participated in the 1970 William Tell exercise held by the US Air Force's Air Defense Command*
(Paul Bennett)

Not part of either the 'first' or 'second' batches of Voodoos delivered to Canada, EF-101B 58-300 (CAF 101067) was actually leased from the US Air Force and assigned to No 414 Sqn at North Bay. The use of modern fast-jet aircraft for the ECM role is nothing new, and for years a variety of aircraft types have been employed to simulate the electronic 'signature' that would be provided by an incoming, hostile Soviet bomber. The best-known machines employed for this special duty were US Air Force EB-57 Canberras.

The all-black EF-101B (again, even the baggage carrier was painted to conform with the scheme) had originally been delivered in the standard CAF finish minus the red and white lightning stripes found on all other CAF Voodoos. (It thus provided evidence that the entire fleet would have looked better without those stripes). Eventually, it appeared in black finish with low visibility national insignia and No 414 Sqn's red and black rudder bars. For a time, the all-black Voodoo had some natural metal evident around its nose, the result of a landing gear accident. Yes, the first and last Voodoos ever in service had suffered landing gear problems!

Sometimes nicknamed the 'Electric Voodoo,' this airframe had taken over the ECM role formerly performed not only by USAF EB-57s but also by Canada's Falcons. It is no secret that the CAF would have liked to possess more of these airplanes, but cost factors and other considerations made it impracticable. In mid-1986, when this narrative was being compiled, the EF-101B was the sole flying Voodoo in the world and was scheduled to be retired virtually at any minute. Given the size and complexity of the Voodoo, as well as its age, it seemed unlikely that any other F-101 airframes would ever fly again.

## The RF-101B

Earlier single-seat Voodoos had been successfully converted to the reconnaissance role (F-101A to RF-101G; F-101C to RF-101H). In the late 1960s, because of the perception that reconnaissance platforms were too few and RF-4C Phantom production too slow, it was decided to conduct a similar conversion programme with ex-Canadian, two-seat Voodoos. Never mind that highly experienced recce pilots could not tolerate the idea of a second crewman in the back seat (one reason why recce Voodoo jocks never adjusted too well to the recce Phantom). Never mind that the number of ex-Canadian airframes was too few to permit a significant and cost-effective programme. Under a contract dated 30 December 1968 awarded to the Martin Marietta Corporation, ex-CAF CF-101Bs from the 'first batch', which retained the inflight refuelling probes of the early interceptor configuration were converted as high/low daylight reconnaissance aircraft under the new designation RF-101B.

These aircraft had been brought back from Canada and had basked in the sun at the Military Aircraft Storage and Disposition Center (MASDC) at Davis-Monthan AFB, Arizona, before being brought out of

TOP LEFT

*Lark One Canada (or in French, Alouette Un Canada, as is painted on the other side of the fuselage) is a CF-101B Voodoo (57-0298, CAF 101014) of No 425 Sqn, seen here at London, Ontario, in June 1984. This machine is one of three painted in bright colours for the 60th anniversary of Canadian military aviation, the others being* Hawk One Canada *(No 409 Sqn) and* Lynx Squadron Canada *(No 416 Sqn)*
*(Douglas R Tachauer)*

*The 'Electric Voodoo,' this EF-101B (57-300; CAF 101067), seen on 27 September 1984, is the last flying Voodoo in the world. The blaze of natural metal on the nose, not an intentional part of the sinister black paint scheme, is the result of a landing gear accident—something that kept happening to the Voodoo, from its first flight to its last*
*(Robbie Shaw)*

mothballs for the RF-101B programme. When modified, these aircraft acquired the KC-135-compatible flying boom refuelling receptacle and had the number two fuselage fuel cell reduced to 433 US gallons (360 Imp gallons), reducing the total fuel tankage in the RF-101B to 2,949 US gallons (2,453 Imp gallons). The resulting airplane, painted in T.O.114 camouflage of the type created for the war in Southeast Asia, seems to have been an extremely expensive tool for a very marginal mission. As noted in Appendix 7, only 22 airframes (plus one developmental machine which was *not* ex-Canadian) were involved in this costly method of developing a recce aircraft which wasn't much use at night or in bad weather.

The missile armament of the CF-101B interceptor was deleted from the RF-101B. Instead, these daylight recce aircraft carried cameras and control equipment in a modified nose which had a distinctive 'square' shape beneath its tip. New communications and navigation equipment was carried in the former weapons bay.

Cameras carried by the only two-seat recce Voodoo included a KS-87B forward camera, a KS-87B left split vertical camera, a KS-87B right split vertical camera, an AXQ-2 forward-looking television camera, and an AXQ-2 downward-looking camera. Most of the instruments in the rear cockpit were removed during the modification. The pilot's cockpit contained a TV viewfinder control indicator. Although a difference in pitot tube lengths for the CF-101B and RF-101B was originally specified, the recce aircraft ended up being the same length as the interceptor.

The RF-101B appears to have been one of the more useless airplanes produced by the Air Force (the Air National Guard, actually) and to have required fix after fix, solely to keep it operating at an acceptable standard. The programme was an attempt to maintain the number of tactical reconnaissance assets in the Air Force at an acceptable, but still relatively minimal, level. The airplanes were all assigned to the 192nd TRS, Nevada Air National Guard, at Reno during the 1971–1972 period, at which time Nevada sent its RF-101Hs to Kentucky and the Kentucky Air National Guard transferred its RF-101Gs to Arkansas, leaving each state unit with only one variant of recce Voodoo.

Thus, the ex-Canadian Voodoos were part of the end of the story, as Voodoos of different variants went out of service at different times.

## The End of the Line

An end had to come to the long career of the 'long bird' as Butterfield had christened it—the aptly-named Voodoo was longer than its Phantom replacement and also had longer legs (range)—and both US and Canadian operations were drawn down over several years. By 1968, the US Air Force had

*The only Voodoo ever on the US civil registry was this F-101B interceptor (57-410),* The Gray Ghost, *registered N8234. The ex-USAF airplane (not one of those used by Canada) was used by Colorado State University and kept at Buckley ANGB, near Denver, for a lengthy series of storm research and other weather programmes (Clyde Gerdes)*

deactivated nine of its F-101B squadrons (13th, 29th, 49th, 75th, 84th, 87th, 98th, 437th and 444th FIS), the airplanes going to the MASDC storage centre while the aircrews were re-cycled to recce Voodoo operations in Southeast Asia. In 1969, three more ADC interceptor squadrons were disbanded (2nd, 59th and 445th FIS), their F-101B Voodoos going to the Maine, North Dakota and Washington Air National Guard units which operated the type. The last five ADC squadrons were phased out in 1970–71, leaving the Air Defense Weapons Center (ADWC) at Tyndall AFB, Florida, as the only active-duty operator of the F-101B. Gradually, the type was replaced in ANG service as well. The 111th FIS of the Texas ANG, as has already been noted, became the last squadron to operate the F-101B Voodoo,

transitioning in 1982 to the F-4C Phantom.

At Tyndall, the 4756th Combat Crew Training Squadron became the 2nd Fighter Interceptor Training Squadron and continued using its F-101B and F-101F aircraft for target-towing and ECM duties. When ADC was disbanded and the Tyndall operation was taken over by Tactical Air Command, this unit became the 82nd Tactical Aerial Towing Squadron, Tyndall was operating B model Voodoos later than anybody else 'south of the border' until 20 September 1982, when Lt Col Bruce A Sanders made the last US operational flight in a Voodoo.

The end of the line for the recce Voodoo came sooner. The 29th TRS at Shaw, like the 4414th CCTS, had become a training unit for the new breed of RF-101C pilots who went to Southeast Asia in the late 1960s. Both squadrons eventually trained Air National Guard pilots who took over their RF-101C airframes.

This narrative will return to North Vietnam, as it must to pay homage to the Voodoo as an 'air combat' machine. Here, however, is the place to make note that the 45th TRS (Polka Dots) at Tan Son Nhut ended a decade of Voodoo combat operations when the last RF-101C departed Saigon on 16 November

1970. No Voodoos were around two years later when the 'Eleven Day War,' known as the Christmas Bombing to some and as Linebacker II to others, brought swarms of B-52 Stratofortresses over the enemy's homeland and wiped out North Vietnam's ability to wage war. Suffice to say, again, that warriors who flew Voodoos contributed to one of the most decisive military victories of modern times—which policymakers who sat at desks then transformed into a defeat.

The 45th TRS's RF-101Cs later served with the Air National Guard at Meridian, Mississippi. The 29th TRS's Voodoos went to the 127th TRG, Michigan Air National Guard, at Selfridge, Mich, Lt Col Roland L Richardson being the last USAF Voodoo squadrom commander when he delivered a recce Voodoo to Selfridge on 28 February 1971.

'I sure will miss that old bird,' Richardson was quoted. The availability of RF-4C Phantom airframes following the wind-down in Southeast Asia spelled *finis* to RF-101 operations and a chapter in history came to an end. 'For some of us, nothing will ever be quite the same,' says Colonel M P Curphey. 'We loved that airplane and we hated it. We cursed it and we praised it. Most of us are better pilots because

it was such a bear to fly. A few of us are not around any longer because it was not always willing to forgive. But it was the biggest, fastest, hottest mother of its era and even after it had grown old, there was nothing else in the sky that could keep up with it.'

## Voodoos on Display

Although the sight of twin J57s on burner slamming a Voodoo through the air will never again grace a battleground or an air show, a serious effort is under way to make certain that the F-101 Voodoo is not lost forever to future generations. In Canada, where the B model interceptor served so valiantly, no fewer than a dozen CF-101B and CF-101F airframes are in storage, divided about evenly between CFB Trenton and CFS Mountain View. All of these machines are from the 'second batch' operated by Canada. Among the survivors in the 'first batch,' no fewer than five ex-Canadians are on display.

CF-101F 59-400 (CAF 17400), which served briefly with the Kentucky Air National Guard as an F-101F (but, in that reconnaissance unit, never as a recce Voodoo) has been on display in Orlando, Florida, wearing the spurious civil registration N37647. CF-101F 59-407 (CAF 17407) made its way to Duluth, Minnesota, where the Air National Guard unit, which once operated the B model, mounted it on an outdoor pylon. CF-101B 59-438 (CAF 17438) is displayed at Tyndall. CF-101B 59-471 (CAF 17471) is on outdoor exhibit at Cresson, Texas in well-intended but slightly inaccurate Canadian markings from the early period, before the RCAF became the CAF. This machine is owned by the Pate Museum. Finally, CF-101B 59-483 (CAF 17483), which was converted to the two-seat RF-101B reconnaissance standard, is on display at Reno, Nevada, with the only Air National Guard unit that ever operated the two-seat recce aircraft.

Reconnaissance Voodoos have also been preserved for display in various locations, as have one or two of the original single-seat strategic fighters. Perhaps the least satisfactory outdoor display is RF-101H 56-0001, the former F-101C strategic fighter which was Robin Olds' 'Balls One' in its heyday and later served in the recce role with the Kentucky Air National Guard. Although a very active group of aviation historians makes its home around the Kentucky Guard's airbase at Standiford Field in Louisville, whoever made the decision to display 56-0001 doesn't seem to have listened to anyone in the group. 'Balls One' has appeared outdoors in a variety of bogus and highly inaccurate Air Force and Air National Guard paint schemes, including the present-day lizard green 'Europe One' scheme which was never, at any time, worn by an operational Voodoo.

## 'Adopt a Voodoo'

Anyone interested in making a personal investment in a Voodoo is reminded that the F-101 is one of the very few aircraft types of which the *original prototype* still survives. After being used as a testbed for the General Electric J79 engine employed by the F-4 Phantom, the original F-101A (53-2418) ended up on display with the Pueblo Historical Society at Pueblo West, Colorado, a hundred miles (160 km) south of Denver. That's right: the *very first* Voodoo still exists! When last seen, it was outdoors in the Colorado air in a paint scheme which appeared not quite realistic.

The director of the non-profit Pueblo museum, William Feder, has made it clear that the folks in Colorado intend to preserve that Voodoo and could use a little help. The refurbishing and preservation of any historical aircraft is a major undertaking, and one which involves considerable work and cost. Fortunately, a cadre of unpaid volunteers has pitched in to keep the first F-101A shipshape. More assistance is needed, however, and anyone interested in this worthy cause should contact retired Lt Col Feder at PO Box 7433, Pueblo West, Colorado 81007, USA.

In another way, the life and times of the Voodoo is being preserved by the people who flew and fought in the roomy cockpit of the RF-101C. A periodic 'Tac Recce Reunion' brings reconnaissance Voodoo pilots and their wives or girlfriends together to relive the days when those J57 engines roared. The most recent reunion was to have been held in October 1986 at Fort

*Canada's replacement for the Voodoo. It was to have been officially called the CF-188 to fit that country's three-digit aircraft designation system and the name Hornet was disavowed because the word is not bilingual in English and French—but this more recent McDonnell product is a CF-18 Hornet anyway. Here, a CF-18 airplane (188716) flies in low-visibility paint scheme in January 1984 (MDC)*

Walton Beach, which is roughly midway between Tyndall and Eglin in the Florida panhandle, and thus ideally situated for a Voodoo get-together. The group is seeking primarily to bring together RF-101A/C pilots who have been out of touch, but it also welcomes contact with those interested in the mission and the aircraft. Anyone with an interest should contact Tac Recce Reunion, PO Box 488, Niceville, Florida 32578.

The guns are still now, the giant J57 engines silent, the sky empty of Voodoos. But in their day, the Voodoo flew and fought like nothing before or since. Because this is an 'Air Combat' series, this narrative now returns to the point at which the first chapter ended—with the Green Pythons of Udorn pitting their RF-101C aircraft against North Vietnam.

# Chapter 8
# The Mention of the Inflight Tankers
## Flying the RF-101C in Combat (II)

'Please make mention of the tankers and rescue crews in your book,' asks Col Ray W Carlson. 'They sure saved more than one of our lives.'

After two years without sitting in a Voodoo cockpit, Lt Col Daniel J (Jack) Nelson went to 'Nam as commander of the 45th TRS (Polka Dots) at Tan Son Nhut. There were no provisions for doing any transition in a combat zone, but Nelson simply couldn't get anyone excited about the fact that he was rusty, even though the regulations said that if one had been out of a particular airplane for one year he *had* to get 'the whole works' to become current. Nelson secured TDY (temporary duty) orders to Shaw and talked the 4414th CCTS (his old squadron) into giving him a simulator ride and three Voodoo flights. This was far from a legal checkout but as soon as he'd gotten seven combat missions under his belt he was properly signed off 'so I could get on with the war.'

By this time, the 45th TRS was being used primarily to support the US Army in South Vietnam. The parent wing, the 460th TRW still under Colonel Ed Taylor, also had two RF-4C Phantom squadrons now, and these performed most of the 'Air Force work,' e.g. missions up North. Nelson didn't have the squadron very long before he was promoted to colonel and almost immediately moved to Director of Operations. It was a bit unusual for a brand-new colonel to hold the all-important DO slot but Ed Taylor (already noted as being astute in choosing the men who fought with him) was an old recce friend who was after the best. As it happened, Nelson and Taylor went together on R & R (rest and recuperation) to Bangkok only to return and find that they had lost an RF-101C to ground fire.

The target, a suspected Triple-A installation, was right up the coast from Tan Son Nhut. Lt Rogers (first name not recalled) went up after it on 3 November 1966 in his RF-101C Voodoo (56-0175). Rogers was hit by something, it was never clear what.

He managed to get out to sea before bailing out and being picked up by a destroyer, and the squadron didn't see him again for a week. He had been fragged over the target at low level, which was unnecessary (Nelson was continually fighting with the Intelligence people to tell his pilots *what* they wanted and not *how* to get it). By becoming a statistic, happily one in the category 'Rescued,' Rogers had confirmed the existence of the Triple-A site even without bringing back any film. Some months thereafter, on 20 June 1967, ten years and 55 days after his first flight in the Voodoo, Jack Nelson completed his final combat mission and went home.

The 45th TRS stayed in the war, as noted in the previous chapter, until 16 November 1970. But it was the Udorn-based Voodoos which seemed to get most of the attention.

### (More) Green Pythons

Lt Col James R Brickel, who inhabited the hooch next to Lt Col John Bull Stirling for some weeks before taking over the 20th TRS from Stirling, was not a member of the old Voodoo fraternity which dated back to the 1950s and could boast years of experience flying recce in Europe. He was, however, yet another future wearer of general's stars—in his case, three. Brickel came to the Green Pythons via a scholarly route and was a kind of thinking man's squadron commander, although no one doubted his determination to lead men into the jaws of hell itself. An aeronautical engineer and Naval Academy graduate, former F-86 Sabre pilot Jim Brickel had worked in the space programme, including the early stages of the Apollo effort. On 10 March 1967, Brickel launched from Udorn in an RF-101C to carry out post-strike recce of the first major strike on the Thai Nguyen steel mill deep in North Vietnam.

The area around Thai Nguyen bristled with 85-

and 90-mm anti-aircraft guns directed by *Fire Can* radars. SAM missile sites were plentiful. Several MiG bases were within easy range. For the first time, waves of F-105 Thunderchiefs and F-4 Phantoms had swarmed down through heavy flak to strike the steel mills. At least one fighter-bomber had been lost and several damaged. It was Brickel's job, that day, to bring home the pictures which would show whether the fighter-bombers had done well or poorly.

Which is why Jim approached Yen Bai, 60 miles (96.5 km) northwest of Hanoi while the raid was still in progress. He was scheduled to arrive over the steel mills in his RF-101C minutes after the last bombs fell. He was accompanied by another RF-101C but it was merely a spare—on this day at least, the preferred method of operating two Voodoos had been overshadowed by the need for fighter escort—and wedged around him was a flight of four F-4C Phantoms from the 8th TFW, Colonel Robin Olds' Ubon-based Wolfpack. Phantom flight leader Lt Col Thomas W McGuire, Jr used his fighters to form a protective screen around Brickel's 'long bird' as they turned northeast toward Thud Ridge and crossed the Red River.

Brickel and McGuire peered at each other across the open reaches of sky. Now, they were being stalked by the *Fan Song* radars associated with SAM missiles. The second RF-101C peeled away, heading out to sea to mate with a tanker, leaving Brickel alone to wield cameras. One Voodoo and four Phantoms swung north of Thud Ridge and turned south. Jim Brickel could see that the target was going to be difficult to pinpoint. The usual low layer of murk clung to the North Vietnamese hills and obscured the valleys, providing a white backdrop for the jets' shadows.

Brickel spotted several columns of smoke rising into the air from the strike on Thai Nguyen. He went through a quick navigation and equipment check. It seemed that the strike force had found the target all right, and he was heading straight toward it—now that North Vietnam's defences had already had plenty of opportunity to zero-in.

Two minutes from his objective, Brickel passed Thud Ridge on schedule and bored toward the target. RED CROWN, the radar picket ship out in the Gulf, began to call out MiG warnings. MiGs were in the air, near the onrushing Voodoo, though none had attacked yet.

Brickel speculated that the MiGs were being recycled because of their earlier efforts against the main strike force. He didn't know. But the Triple-A threat was very real. Hundreds of guns opened up on the Voodoo and its Phantom escort as they came into view south of the cloud bank.

F-4C flight leader McGuire was later quoted by Major Jimmy W Kilbourne in *The Airman* magazine:

'Flak bursts filled the air but, fortunately, the fuses on the 37- and 57-mm shells were set a few thousand feet below us. I would guess that they had been set at normal bomb release altitude for the strike aircraft. Anyway, I had never seen that much flak except in World War 2 movies.

'Then it happened! The radar-controlled 85-mm

*Members of the 20th TRS (Green Pythons) at Udorn, Thailand commemorate 7,100 combat missions between 1 April 1966 and 27 October 1967. Under its two commanders, Lt Col John Bull Stirling and Lt Col James R Brickel, the squadron also suffered ten RF-101C Voodoos lost in combat (Garrison)*

guns opened fire. We knew that those guns could quickly adjust their flak patterns to our changes in airspeed, altitude and headings. We also knew that their task would be an easy one when Colonel Brickel's RF-101C rolled out in straight and level flight before reaching the steel mills . . .'

It was Jim Brickel's turn in the Barrel. As he entered the flak-filled sky over the Thai Nguyen steel works, Brickel was very much aware that strike aircraft had already taken hits there, and that he was completely alone with the terrible responsibility of bringing home the pictures of their work. He also knew that the gunners below had taken the mark of his Voodoo and were concentrating on him. Nevertheless, he held his RF-101C steady and unwavering as it neared the target.

McGuire saw an 85-mm shell explode directly beneath the Voodoo. It was like a red splash of watercolour. The Phantom pilot fully expected the RF-101C to begin disintegrating in mid-air. In fact, the large access door to the right J57 engine did peel off the underbelly and sail through the formation of Phantoms. Then the Voodoo's right aileron made a cracking sound and blew away.

The 85-mm Triple-A shell, perhaps a foot (30 cm) long with the diameter of a baseball had exploded under the right engine. It nearly sent the RF-101C spiralling out of control over the steel mills. Inside the cockpit, Brickel was slammed around with violent force. He fought desperately with the controls, at the same time struggling against powerful G forces pressing against his body. With a near-superhuman effort, he succeeded in righting the aircraft just as the cameras started clicking away.

It was a remarkable sight. The RF-101C Voodoo, leaving pieces of itself in its own slipstream, sputtering and burning, trying to run amok whilst Jim Brickel held the crippled craft straight and level

throughout the photo run. 85-mm flak now swirled around him, some of it seemingly close enough to reach out and touch. Brickel was in immediate danger of an engine fire or explosion and if that didn't happen the North Vietnamese might yet score a dead-centre hit. Three of McGuire's four Phantoms also took hits from the 85-mm barrage.

The RF-101C did slow down by about 100 mph (160 km/h) but all five aircraft managed to complete the run-in, swing back to safety, and egress North Vietnam. The Voodoo made it back to Udorn with the pictures!

Phantom pilot McGuire, who flew 100 missions up North and won the Silver Star and Distinguished Flying Cross later said of his colleague in the Voodoo, 'that flak around Colonel Brickel's RF-101 was the worst I saw in North Vietnam. I never expected all five aircraft to get out of there—least of all Colonel Brickel's.'

The mission resulted in award of the Air Force Cross, the second highest American decoration for valour, making Jim Brickel the highest-decorated Voodoo pilot of the conflict. The citation accompanying the medal read in part, 'Despite a direct hit by anti-aircraft fire that extensively damaged his aircraft, Colonel Brickel continued to the target and acquired 100 per cent photographic coverage. He then made a successful withdrawal from hostile territory on a single engine and landed at his home base.'

Jim Brickel was only beginning. On 1 May 1967, the day before he relieved Stirling as 20th TRS commander, he led a flight of two unarmed and unescorted RF-101Cs to Hoa Loc airfield, an especially dangerous location which usually swarmed with MiGs, and he obtained one hundred per cent photographic coverage despite having to evade two SAMs. For this mission, Brickel earned the

LEFT
*Voodoo as seen from Voodoo. This RF-101C recce craft
(56-0063) was photographed by a wingman in a two-ship
formation over Laos, heading towards targets in North
Vietnam. Camouflaged Voodoo belonged to the 20th TRS
(Green Pythons) based at Udorn, Thailand
(*courtesy Col Ray W Carlson*)*

*Although no photos are known to exist of the 10 March
1967 mission which earned him the Air Force Cross and
made him the highest-decorated Voodoo pilot, Lt Col
James R Brickel was, on occasion, caught by the camera
while going in harm's way. By now commander of the 20th
TRS, Brickel pilots this RF-101C over Hoa Loc, North
Vietnam in May 1967. Camouflage blends nicely with
background
(*Brickel*)*

*Pilots of the 20th TRS, the Green Pythons, then commanded by Lt Col James R Brickel, at Udorn on 31 May 1967*
*(Brickel)*

BELOW
*Lt Col James R Brickel (left), whose 10 March 1967 Air Force Cross mission makes him the highest-decorated Voodoo pilot, stands at 20th TRS headquarters, Udorn, with Captain Ray W Carlson. Brickel is now a retired lieutenant general in Oakton, Virginia, while Carlson is a retired colonel in Grand Junction, Colorado*
*(Carlson)*

Distinguished Flying Cross. On 21 May 1967 (not 22 May, as Air Force records show), he led two unarmed and unescorted RF-101C Voodoos on a bomb damage assessment mission to a target near Hanoi. The RF-101Cs encountered heavy flak and intense SAM barrages. Again, 100 per cent photo coverage was attained and this time Brickel received the Silver Star.

Jim Brickel flew 106 missions over North Vietnam in the RF-101C before returning stateside in September 1967. Not every one of the Udorn-based Voodoo pilots made it home. Major Notley G Maddox did not.

Years later, men look back and remember. Some who flew up north not only didn't come back, they were never even accounted for. The myth persists that among the few MIA (missing in action) for whom North Vietnam has failed to provide such accounting, some Americans *may* remain alive. This myth is, to the wives and children of the men we left behind, a cruel and heartless joke—perpetuated, in part, by silly and senseless Hollywood productions. The fact remains, Hanoi knows more than it has told, and an accounting is now a decade overdue.

## Mission to Kep

Ray Carlson remembers:

'I was Major Notley G Maddox's wingman on 20 May 1967, the day he was lost [in RF-101C 56-120 of the 20th TRS] near Kep airfield [a major North Vietnamese MiG base]. Our target was the Kep army barracks which was just to the south of the airfield.

We had a late takeoff with TOT [time over target] being around 1600 hours.

'I knew Notley at Shaw and again at Udorn. I knew him only through flying and work as he was a very quiet individual and kept very much to himself. As I understand, he was within a few hours of having his PhD in physics. Most of his free time at Udorn was spent reading and studying. I never met any of his family, but can say he was a very devoted family man. In Air Force terms, he was a great guy with some bad luck too early in his life.

'The day of the mission was spent doing the routine flight planning, intelligence briefing, and keeping an eye on the weather. Our takeoff, being as late as it was in the afternoon, gave plenty of time for thunderstorms to build. We had to get through a severe line of them in RP-1 [Route Package One, i.e., the southernmost part of North Vietnam]. From Udorn we departed on an NE heading out over the coast about twenty to thirty miles [32 to 48 km] offshore, then headed north to where RED CROWN was anchored. We let down and ingressed on the deck just north of Haiphong Ridge. At the west end of the ridge we lit the burners and popped to about 15,000 feet [4572 m]. Our flight plan called for us to turn to a southwesterly heading initially and to make the bad guys think we were headed for the Northeast Railroad Line and Hanoi, and then come back around hard to an easterly heading descending to egress on the deck north of Haiphong Ridge.

'Notley turned to the southwest, but came back to the north a bit too soon and rolled out to the east side of the barracks. I was thrown wide in the turn and a bit behind, but with a slight correction I lined up beautifully on the target. I called Notley and advised him of the situation. At this point, I had visual contact with him, and he established a visual on me. I advised him to join on me, that I was lined up on the target.

He acknowledged. I next started my photo run. The next transmission I heard from Notley was that he was over Kep and had been hit, but it was only a little one. The words that it was only a little one have stuck in my mind. I came to the conclusion that he personally had been hit. After hearing his call, I took my head out of the viewfinder to look for him. We had lost visual contact and the flak over Kep was thick enough to walk on. I advised that I had the target coverage and to egress. Notley acknowledged, and indicated that he was turning to an easterly heading. My last radio contact with Notley was over the west end of the Haiphong Ridge. I saw no chute, heard no beeper [survival radio], and saw no smoke to indicate an aircraft down. I maintained around 10–12 thousand feet [3048–3657 m] on my way out, but was unable to re-estabish radio contact. Once over the coast, I contacted RED CROWN and advised what had happened. They indicated they were showing a bogie high and in my six o'clock position. About five minutes later, RED CROWN reported losing the bogie. I show Notley as MIA [missing in action] at 1620 local. Being late in the day, there was nothing else airborne bearing US markings, in RP-6 [Route Package Six, the area around Hanoi] or nearby. Jim Brickel, now our squadron commander, met me when I landed. I debriefed Jim and from there we went to the wing commander. To the best of my

*The Vietnam war produced camouflage and tailcodes. The Voodoo was the first warplane with the former, and one of the last with the latter, which are properly called tactical unit identifiers. The AH on the fin of RF-101C (56-0061), seen taking off from Tan Son Nhut, identifies it as belonging to the 45th TRS, the Polka Dots. This was the final squadron to employ Voodoos in combat* (Robert Burgess)

knowledge, nothing was ever turned up on Notley.' Although Maddox has subsequently been officially listed as killed in action, the settlement which ended the Vietnam war requires an accounting from Hanoi which has never been satisfactorily provided.

## The 'Heated Up' War

Ray Carlson began *his* tour with the Green Pythons on 26 December 1966, and thus serves as a 'bridge' between the events in chapter one and the later fighting described in this chapter. 'At the time I arrived, guys from the 20th TRS were being lost at the rate of one per week. Not very good odds.' Carlson had great respect for the RF-101C Voodoo, for its oft-mentioned stability as a flying platform, and for its toughness. He believed in the doctrine which called for sending RF-101Cs into Route Package Six in pairs. One purpose was to find out what had been causing the losses of solo airplanes—whether it was MiGs, SAMs, Triple-A or automatic weapons. In fact, it turned out to be all, but until that time the cause of most individual losses was unknown—and no accurate record has ever been assembled.

Beginning in about April 1967, Carlson and his wingman also launched an airborne spare in addition to paired Voodoos on every mission into the Hanoi-Haiphong region. 'With just two aircraft, if one aborted the other was required to abort and the mission was lost.' Carlson recalls one occasion when there were differing opinions about thunderstorms—one officer insisting that 'thunderstorms are soft, lots of water, and that was it.' In fact, the thunderstorms were as much a part of life for Voodoo pilots as the North Vietnamese. At one point, when nine RF-101Cs were out of commission with hail damage, the decision was made not to press on when a mission involved flying through a tropical storm.

'Things really started heating up about March of 1967 and 90 per cent of our missions were scheduled for RP-6. Also, along about March we started planning our missions to pick up additional targets in the prime target area. The thinking behind this was if you were in the area and could get additional targets, you might not have to go back the next day. So they started fragging us for more than one target. As an example, Bob Wolfe and I, on 17 June 1967, were fragged for the Northeast Railroad from Kep with a flight of F-4s for escort. Bob was lead and I was wingman. I picked up 34 targets. I don't remember the number Bob acquired. We had fifteen SAMs fired at us. So it was a wild ride.'

Carlson, like every RF-101C jock, praises the other friendly airmen who contributed to the Voodoo effort. Air rescue people were held in high regard. It was Carlson, among many other RF-101C pilots, who insisted on the mention of the inflight tankers. On at least one occasion, a Voodoo with battle damage was 'eating up' fuel faster than the KC-135

*Captain Ray Carlson (right) gets champagne and flowers at Udorn for completing his 100 missions over North Vietnam, and is grinning at having survived the war. Captain Charles C (Chuck) Winston III (left) did neither (Carlson)*

RIGHT
*Captain Chuck Winston's immediate superior found time between RF-101C missions to begin work on his OER, the AF Form 77 or 'Company Grade Officer Effectiveness Report.' This is a rough draft of the report which, when finished, would have gone into Winston's 201 file (personnel file). At the controls of RF-101C Voodoo 56-0207 on 1 August 1967, Chuck Winston was killed in action (Carlson)*

## V. OVER-ALL EVALUATION (Compare this officer ONLY with officers of the same grade.)

| UNSATIS-FACTORY | MARGINAL | BELOW AVERAGE | EFFECTIVE AND COMPETENT | VERY FINE | EXCEPTIONALLY FINE | OUTSTANDING |
|---|---|---|---|---|---|---|
| ☐ | ☐ | ☐ | ☐ | ☐ | ☐ | ☐ |

SPECIFIC JUSTIFICATION REQUIRED FOR THESE SECTIONS

SPECIFIC JUSTIFICATION REQUIRED FOR THESE SECTIONS

## VI. PROMOTION POTENTIAL

| | |
|---|---|
| 1. DOES NOT DEMONSTRATE A CAPABILITY FOR PROMOTION AT THIS TIME. ☐ | 2. PERFORMING WELL IN PRESENT GRADE. SHOULD BE CONSIDERED FOR PROMOTION ALONG WITH CONTEMPORARIES. ☐ |
| 3. DEMONSTRATES CAPABILITIES FOR INCREASED RESPONSIBILITY. CONSIDER FOR ADVANCEMENT AHEAD OF CONTEMPORARIES. ☐ | 4. OUTSTANDING GROWTH POTENTIAL BASED ON DEMONSTRATED PERFORMANCE. PROMOTE WELL AHEAD OF CONTEMPORARIES. ☐ |

## VII. COMMENTS

FACTS AND SPECIFIC ACHIEVEMENTS: Captain Winston is a highly competent and motivated officer. He has demonstrated exceptional capability as a combat reconnaissance pilot and flight leader in SEA. Irrespective of the lack of previous experience in the RF 101 prior to combat crew training, he readily adapted to the combat environment and subsequently has completed 3 3 reconnaissance missions on formidable targets over North Vietnam. He is a very meticulous and thorough flight planner, assuring every aspect is covered to acquire the target. His flight debriefings with intelligence are always precise and accurate, with time, position, and heading being exact. Consequently his missions have produced outstanding photographs of primary targets which has been of great value in assessing damage and selecting future targets. Inspite of frequent commitment against difficult targets, he has maintained very high morale. His overall contribution to the squadron in accomplishing its mission in SEA has been outstanding. In addition to his primary duty Captain Winston performed the additional duty of squadron ASSISTANT awards and decorations officer in a highly effective manner. In this capacity he has worked many additional hours writing and seeing those who are deserving receive their just award. He has personally written all Air Medal awards and nearly half of all other awards to be presented squadron members since assuming the duty. STRENGTHS: Captain Winston is a very eager person and willingly accepts any job or responsibility given him. He is X mature for his age and experience and is an exceptionally fine team member. He possesses excellent communicative abilities, both oral and written. SUGGESTED ASSIGNMENTS: Captain Winston is XXX an exceptionally fine pilot and should continue as a crew member in a tactical unit. He should be afforded the opportunity for input into the Air Force Squadron Officers School. OTHER COMMENTS: Officer has performed duty in SEA throughout the period of this report.

## VIII. REPORTING OFFICIAL

| NAME, GRADE, AFSN, AND ORGANIZATION | DUTY TITLE | | SIGNATURE *Ray Carlson* |
|---|---|---|---|
| | AERO RATING | CODE | DATE |

## IX. REVIEW BY INDORSING OFFICIAL

| NAME, GRADE, AFSN, AND ORGANIZATION | DUTY TITLE | | SIGNATURE |
|---|---|---|---|
| | AERO RATING | CODE | DATE |

U.S. GOVERNMENT PRINTING OFFICE : 1964 O—736-718

Stratotanker could replace it—so the '135 simply headed for home with the Voodoo attached to its refuelling boom! 'We also loved to have the F-4 Phantoms with us in RP-6 except that *we had to throttle back* [emphasis added]. Normally we ran at over 500 knots [710 km/h] indicated airspeed while making our photo run in RP-6, but with the Phantoms we had to throttle back to around 420 to 450 knots [580 to 670 km/h] in order for the Phantoms to keep up with us.' It is worth repeating that the McDonnell RF-101C Voodoo flew the *fastest* combat missions ever undertaken on this planet, in an era when it was being discovered that speed was not all-important for many missions.

And, adds Carlson, 'yes, every time we headed up to RP-6, it was referred to as "your turn in the Barrel."' Why did they use those precise words? Carlson does not answer.

By now, it should be obvious. Those who know don't ask. Those who ask don't know.

## The Highest Price

When Lyndon Johnson ended the bombing of North Vietnam on 31 October 1967, it ended the saga of Voodoo operations 'up North' although, as has been noted, the 45th TRS in particular continued to fly recce sorties in support of the US Army in South Vietnam. By the time a second aerial campaign was mounted north of the 17th Parallel in 1972, Voodoos were no longer 'in theatre,' but their contribution was far from forgotten. Always far fewer in number than the better known Thuds, Phantoms and Stratoforts, the RF-101C Voodoos made a contribution that was out of all proportion to their numbers. Long after the RF-4C Phantom was the principal tactical recce bird in Southeast Asia, so long as Voodoos remained, Voodoos were given the toughest and most difficult jobs. Colonel Kent Harbaugh, the US Air Attaché at the American Embassy in London, flew RF-4Cs from the beginning and operated with the wing at Tan Son Nhut that had once been commanded by Ed Taylor. Harbaugh got himself into some pretty bad scrapes and escaped by the narrowest of margins. But while he was flying RF-4Cs over South Vietnam, Laos and Cambodia, the *only* recce aircraft going 'up North' were from the companion squadron—the ubiquitous Polka Dots and their RF-101Cs. The RF-4C weenies took over the recce commitment up North only after the Voodoos were withdrawn.

While young men (and a few not so young) were always willing to risk everything by taking the Voodoo into battle, old men like me seemed unable to improve a world in which conflict is perpetual and the challenge to liberty is unending. In the final years of the twentieth century, the only issue of importance is whether free men possess the will to employ force of arms when need is. A *few* examples of recent success come to mind—Entebbe, the Falklands—but for us Americans there is ground to fear that, when it's

*Captain Charles C (Chuck) Winston III, RF-101C Voodoo pilot, 20th Tactical Reconnaissance Squadron, shortly before his final mission up North* (Carlson)

TOP RIGHT
*Major Bobby Bagley (right) was regarded as one of the best pilots ever to climb into a Voodoo. Bagley belonged to the 20th TRS at Udorn and was killed in combat on 16 September 1967 while flying RF-101C 56-180. He was the last Voodoo pilot to die in combat in Southeast Asia* (Carlson)

RIGHT
*Even after the RF-101C had been retired from the combat zone, recce pilots still trained in the airplane. RF-101C Voodoo (56-0161) of the 31st TRS at Shaw AFB, South Carolina, on 3 June 1970. The distinctive checked design on the tail consists of alternating red and black colours* (Norman Taylor)

needed most, the will won't be there. Voodoo pilots, navigators and maintenance men lived in a world where every able male was expected to serve his time in uniform and every generation was given a war to win; a few people in a more recent era no longer see armed service as necessary, let alone honourable, and may have contributed to the *many* recent examples—Frequent Wind, Desert One, Beirut—where we failed and lost. The Voodoo may not have brought a *pax Americana*, but it guarded freedom and it won battles. And it was maintained and flown, always, by men who *were* willing and who knew the price. A wing commander in Southeast Asia, commenting on a brave action by one of his pilots, was heard to say it beneath his breath. 'God help us when no such men are left.'

Captain Charles C (Chuck) Winston III was an RF-101C Voodoo jock with the Udorn-based Green Pythons and a member of a generation which understood freedom, understood tyranny. He was a member of Ray Carlson's flight in the 20th TRS. 'Chuck was a super young officer and jock. Chuck had a very positive attitude towards everything and regardless of what you asked him to do, it was always, "YES, SIR!" He loved to fly. He knew how to have a good time. On my 95th or 96th mission, I was scheduled as the airborne spare on a mission to Hanoi with Major Homer Hunt and Chuck. About this time, I was sweating missions looking for number 100. As we were heading out to the aircraft, Chuck looked at me and with his typical grin, which he always used, said, "Hey don't sweat it. Homer and I aren't going to abort."' Chuck Winston seems to have been upbeat and positive about everything around him. If they said it couldn't be done, he searched for a way. If they said the news was bad, he looked for a silver lining. He was a believer, an optimist.' Ray Carlson completed his own 100 missions. But, 'Chuck was shot down two days after I had completed my tour and gone to Bangkok. I learned of it while I was there.' Winston's death, deep in North Vietnam, was confirmed but it will never be known how the enemy got him.

So there is sadness in the Voodoo story, just as there is humour. But above all, there is greatness. The Voodoo was created, flew, and fought in an era when men and airplanes possessed greatness. Finally, the Voodoo story must possess, in addition to tragedy and triumph, at least a small hint of mystery. After all, McDonnell fighters are usually given names which reek of mystery.

In 1986, as these pages were going to press, I visited RAF Bentwaters, England—now home of an A-10 Warthog wing, but once the location of the thundering Voodoos flown by Bob Hanson, Robin Olds, and others in possession of greatness. In the East Anglia sunshine, long after no Voodoo was supposed to be left, I glanced down Bentwaters' flight line and saw . . . a Voodoo. It was a very real Voodoo, all right. What's more, although no F-101B had ever taken to the air from any airbase in the British Isles, it was a very real F-101B interceptor, the paint peeling from its outdated markings of the 111th FIS, Texas Air National Guard. No Voodoo was flying anywhere, but it was there and it was real.

I knew. But I asked anyway.

'Oh, that's just a visitor on the transient line,' an airman said.

He was wrong. The F-101B was a non-flyable airframe, one of a number which have recently been brought to Europe, minus engines, avionics and other equipment, to serve as battle damage repair ground trainers. The Voodoo at Bentwaters is teaching men how to fix and turn around the A-10, F-15 and F-16 combat planes of today.

Mystery? When we started down the long road which produced this volume, I asked Ed O'Neil, veteran of many missions over Hanoi, why those precise words. 'You know, about it being your turn in the Barrel?'

Later, Ed told me, of course. But first he said, 'Just mentioning the phrase, "it's your turn in the Barrel" will key anyone who knows the story and they will relate to the full meaning of what kind of mission was being flown.' I was delighted, at Bentwaters, to see that battle damage trainer and to know that the F-101 Voodoo has not bowed out, not yet, from its long tour of duty in the United States Air Force. So the story is not finished and, for a few readers at least, this segment of it will end with the question unanswered.

*Only Norman Taylor's camera could record such a definitive version of the final, Southeast Asia paint scheme employed on the 'long bird.' Still wearing the camouflage and tailcode of the 45th TRS (Polka Dots) in Saigon, from which it has just returned, RF-101C Voodoo (56-0119) has now been assigned to the Air National Guard in Meridian, Mississippi, when seen on 13 November 1971* (Norman Taylor)

189

# Glossary

AAA — Anti-aircraft artillery fire. Also: Triple-A
AFB — Air Force Base
CFB — Canadian Forces Base
CIA — Central Intelligence Agency
Cr — Crashed
DMZ — Demilitarized Zone
ECM — Electronic countermeasures
G — One gravity force
MIA — Missing in Action
NACA — National Advisory Committee for Aeronautics (renamed NASA in 1958)
NASA — National Aeronautics and Space Administration
NATO — North Atlantic Treaty Organization
NVN — North Vietnam
POW — Prisoner of War
SAM — Surface-to-air missile, usually referring to Soviet SA-2 *Guideline*
SVN — South Vietnam

# Appendices

## Appendix 1: **F-101 Voodoos Manufactured**

| Model | Amount | From | To | Remarks |
|---|---|---|---|---|
| F-101A | 29 | 53-2418 | 53-2446 | 29 converted to RF-101G |
|  | 48 | 54-1438 | 54-1485 |  |
| *Subtotal* | 77 |  |  |  |
| YRF-101A | 2 | 54-149 | 54-150 | Initially scheduled as F-101A |
| *Subtotal* | 2 |  |  |  |
| RF-101A | 28 | 54-1494 | 54-1521 | Approx 8 transferred to Republic of China |
|  | 7 | 56-155 | 56-161 |  |
| *Subtotal* | 35 |  |  |  |
| NF-101B | 1 | 56-232 |  | F-101B prototype |
| *Subtotal* | 1 |  |  |  |
| F-101B | 96 | 56-233 | 56-328 | Includes approx 79 TF-101B/F-101F |
|  | 206 | 57-247 | 57-452 | 112 CF-101B, 20 CF-101F transferred to Canada |
|  | 84 | 58-259 | 58-342 | 22 ex-Canadian CF-101B converted to RF-101B |
|  | 93 | 59-391 | 59-483 | 1 converted to NF-101B (57-409) |
| *Subtotal* | 479 |  |  |  |
| F-101C | 8 | 54-1486 | 54-1493 | 32 converted to RF-101H |
|  | 39 | 56-1 | 56-39 |  |
| *Subtotal* | 47 |  |  |  |
| RF-101C | 96 | 56-40* | 56-135* | Initially scheduled as F-101C |
|  | 70 | 56-162 | 56-231 |  |
| *Subtotal* | 166 |  |  |  |
| **Total** | 807 |  |  |  |

## Appendix 2: **F-101B Dual Control Equipment Airplanes**★

| | | |
|---|---|---|
| F-101B-70-MC | 56-274, 56-275, 56-275, *56-277* | 4 |
| F-101B-75-MC | 56-289, 56-294, 56-299 | 3 |
| F-101B-80-MC | *56-304*, 56-308, 56-312, 56-316, 56-320, *56-324*, *56-328* | 7 |
| F-101B-85-MC | 57-263, 57-267, 57-271, 57-275, 57-279, 57-283, 57-287, 57-292, 57-297, 57-302, 57-307 | 11 |
| F-101B-90-MC | 57-312, 57-317, *57-322*, 57-327, *57-332*, 57-337, 57-342, 57-347, 57-352, 57-357 | 10 |
| F-101B-95-MC | 57-365, 57-372, 57-379, 57-486, 57-393, *57-400*, 57-407 | 7 |
| F-101B-100-MC | 57-414, 57-421, 57-428, 57-449 | 4 |
| F-101B-105-MC | 58-262, 58-269, 58-276, 58-283, 58-290, 58-297 | 6 |
| F-101B-110-MC | 58-304, 58-311, 58-318, 58-324, 58-331, 58-338 | 6 |
| F-101B-115-MC | *59-393*, *59-400*, *59-407*, 59-413, *59-419*, 59-425, *59-437* | 6 |
| F-101B-120-MC | *59-443*, 59-449, *59-454*, *59-460*, *59-466*, 56-472, 59-478 | 7 |
| **Total** | | 72 |

★As manufactured. Airframes 1–58 initially designated TF-101B; airframes 59-72 initially designated TF-101F, but 1–72 identified by McDonnell simply as 'F-101B dual control equipment airplanes.' 152 more airframes were converted to dual controls after manufacture. On 3 February 1961, all dual-control aircraft were redesignated F-101F. Ten airframes *underlined* were delivered to Canada in first batch and redesignated CF-101F. The ten airframes delivered to Canada in the second batch included the seven airframes with broken *underlining*, plus three airframes (56-253, 56-260, 56-262) not initially manufactured with dual controls.

## Appendix 3: **F-101B Voodoos Delivered to Canada (First Batch)**★

| | | | |
|---|---|---|---|
| F-101B-115-MC | 59-391/411 | RCAF 17391/17411 | 21 |
| | 59-433/440 | 17433/17440 | 8 |
| F-101B-120-MC | 59-441/453 | 17441/17453 | 13 |
| | 59-455/457 | 17455/17457 | 3 |
| | 59-459/461 | 17459/17461 | 3 |
| | 59-463/464 | 17463/17464 | 2 |
| | 59-466/472 | 17466/17472 | 7 |
| | 59-475/483 | 17475/17483 | 9 |
| Total | | | 66 |

★Designated CF-101B in Canadian service. Includes 10 F-101B dual-control equipment airplanes designated CF-101F in Canadian service, these bing 59-393, 59-400, 59-437, 50-443, 59-449, 59-460, 49-466, 59-472, 59-478. Includes 22 Canadian CF-101B airframes later converted to RF-101B configuration and listed separately. 66 delivered to Canada beginning October 1961; 56 survivors returned to US custody in 1971.

## Appendix 4: **F-101B Voodoos Delivered to Canada (Second Batch)**★

| | | | |
|---|---|---|---|
| F-101B-60-MC | 56-253 | CAF 101001 | 1 |
| F-101B-65-MC | 56-260, 56-262 | 101002/101003 | 2 |
| F-101B-70-MC | 56-277 | 101004 | 1 |
| F-101B-80-MC | 56-304, 56-324, 56-328 | 101005/101007 | 3 |
| F-101B-85-MC | 57-268, 57-273, 57-286, 57-289, 57-293, 57-296, 57-298/299, 57-303, 57-305/306 | 101008/101018 | 11 |
| F-101B-90-MC | 57-314/315, 57-321/323, 57-332, 57-334, 57-340/341, 57-346, 57-351, 57-354 | 101019/101030 | 12 |
| F-101B-95-MC | 57-358/360, 57-362/364, 57-366, 57-368/369, 57-373/375, 57-380/382, 57-384, 57-388, 57-391, 57-395/396, 57-398, 57-400 | 101031/101052 | 22 |
| F-101B-100-MC | 57-418, 57-420, 57-424, 57-426, 57-429, 57-431/434, 57-441/444, 57-451 | 101053/101066 | 14 |
| Total | | | 66 |

★Designated CF-101B in Canadian Service. Includes 10 F-101B dual-control equipment airplanes designated CF-101F in Canadian service, these being 56-253, 56-260, 56-262, 56-277, 56-304, 56-324, 56-328, 57-322, 57-332, 57-400. 66 delivered to Canada beginning in 1971. In addition, aircraft F-101B-105-MC 58-300 (CAF 101067) leased from USAF as EC-101B.

## Appendix 5: **F-101A Voodoos Converted to RF-101G***

| | | |
|---|---|---|
| F-101A-25-MC | 54-1445, 54-1449, 54-1451/1452 | 4 |
| F-101A-30-MC | 54-1453/1455. 54-1457, 54-1459/1464 | 10 |
| F-101A-35-MC | 54-1466, 54-1468, 54-1470, 54-1472/1473, 54-1475/1477, 54-1479, 54-1481/1482, 54-1484/1485 | 13 |
| Total | | 27 |

*Some reports list a total of 29 aircraft, possibly including 54-1456, 54-1469 and/or 54-1516 as the two additional machines.

## Appendix 6: **F-101C Voodoos converted to RF-101H**

| | | |
|---|---|---|
| F-101C-40-MC | 54-1486/1488, 54-1491, 54-1493, 56-0001/0004, 56-0006 | 10 |
| F-101C-45-MC | 56-0010/0011, 56-0012, 56-0014, 56-0016, 56-0018/0019 | 7 |
| F-101C-50-MC | 56-0020, 56-0022/0023, 56-0025/0027, 56-0019/0036, 56-0039 | 15 |
| Total | | 32 |

## Appendix 7: **CF-101B Voodoos converted to RF-101B**

| | | |
|---|---|---|
| F-101B-85-MC | 57-301* | 1 |
| F-101B-115-MC | 59-391, 59-397, 59-398, 59-402, 59-403, 59-404, 59-410, 59-434, 59-436 | 9 |
| F-101B-120-MC | 59-441, 59-447, 59-448, 59-450, 59-453, 59-457, 59-459, 59-463, 59-467, 59-477, 59-481, 59-482, 59-483 | 13 |
| Total | | 23 |

*57-301 was a developmental test airframe and had not previously served in Canada.

## Appendix 8: **Voodoo Variants**

| | | |
|---|---|---|
| XF-88 | Penetration fighter prototype | 1 built |
| XF-88A | Penetration fighter with afterburner | 1 built |
| XF-88B | Turboprop testbed | (1 converted) |
| F-101A | Strategic fighter 6.33Gs | 77 built |
| JF-101A | Developmental test aircraft | (7 converted) |
| YRF-101A | Reconnaissance prototypes | 2 built |
| RF-101A | Reconnaissance aircraft 6.33Gs | 35 built |
| F-101B | Interceptor | 479 built |
| CF-101B | Canadian interceptor | (112 transferred) |
| JF-101B | Developmental aircraft | (1 converted) |
| NF-101B | Developmental aircraft | 1 built, (1 converted) |
| RF-101B | Reconnaissance conversion of F-101B | (23 converted) |
| TF-101B | Dual-control equipment airplane | (72 + built or conv) |
| EF-101B | Canadian ECM aircraft | (1 transferred) |
| F-101C | Strategic fighter 7.33Gs | 39 built |
| F-101D | Designation not used | (not built) |
| F-101E | Designation not used | (not built) |
| F-101F | Initially interceptors; later dual-control | (72 + built or conv) |
| CF-101F | Canadian dual-control equipment airplanes | (20 transferred) |
| TF-101F | alternate desig. for dual-control airplanes | (72 + built or conv) |
| RF-101C | Reconnaissance aircraft 7.33Gs | 166 built |
| RF-101G | Reconnaissance conversion of F-101A | (27 converted) |
| RF-101H | Reconnaissance conversion of F-101C | (32 converted) |
| XF-109 | Designation considered by USAF for F-101B | (not built) |

## Appendix 9: **F-101 Voodoo Squadrons**

*Air Research and Development Command (ARDC)*

| | | |
|---|---|---|
| 3421 TS | Eglin AFB, Fla | RF-101A |

*Air Defense Command/Aerospace Defense Command (ADC)*

| | | |
|---|---|---|
| 2 FIS | Suffolk County AB, NY | F-101B/F |
| 2 FITS | Tyndall AFB, Fla | F-101B/F, NF-101B |
| 13 FIS | Glasgow AFB, Montana | F-101B/F |
| 15 FIS | Davis-Monthan AFB, Ariz | F-101B/F |
| 18 FIS | Grand Forks AFB, ND | F-101B/F |
| 29 FIS | Malmstrom AFB, Montana | F-101B/F |
| 49 FIS | Griffiss AFB, NY | F-101B/F |
| 60 FIS | Otis, AFB, Mass | F-101B/F |
| 62 FIS | K I Sawyer AFB, Mich | F-101B/F |
| 75 FIS | Dow AFB, Maine | F-101B/F |
| 83 FIS | Hamilton AFB, Calif | F-101B/F |
| 84 FIS | Hamilton AFB, Calif | F-101B/F |
| 87 FIS | Lockbourne AFB, Ohio | F-101B/F |
| 98 FIS | Dover AFB, Delaware | F-101B/F |
| 322 FIS | Kingsley Field, Oregon | F-101B/F |
| 437 FIS | Oxnard AFB, Calif | F-101B/F |
| 444 FIS | Char eston AFB, SC | F-101B/F |
| 445 FIS | Wurtsmith AFB, Mich | F-101B/F |
| 4750 TS | Tyndall AFB, Fla | F-101B/F |
| 4756 ADS/ | | |
| 4756 CCTS | Tyndall AFB, Fla | F-101B/F |

*Air National Guard (ANG)*

| | | |
|---|---|---|
| 111 FIS | Ellington AFB, Texas | F-101B/F |
| 116 FIS | Spokane, Washington | F-101B/F |
| 123 FIS | Portland, Oregon | F-101B/F |
| 132 FIS | Bangor AFB, Maine | F-101B/F |
| 136 FIS | Niagara Falls, NY | F-101B/F |
| 178 FIS | Fargo, ND | F-101B/F |
| 179 FIS | Duluth, Minnesota | F-101B/F |
| 154 TRS | Little Rock, Arkansas | RF-101A/C/H |
| 165 TRS | Louisville, Kentucky | F-101F/RF-101C/G |
| 192 TRS | Reno, Nevada | RF-101B/H |
| 186 TRS | Meridian, Miss | RF-101C |
| 127 TRG | Selfridge ANGB, Mich | RF-101A/C |

*Royal Canadian Air Force/Canadian Armed Forces (RCAF/CAF)*

| | | |
|---|---|---|
| 409 Sqn | CFB Comox/CFB Cold Lake | CF-101B/F |
| 410 Sqn | CFB Uplands/CFB Bagotville | CF-101B/F |
| 414 Sqn | CFB North Bay | CF-101B/F/EF-101B |
| 416 Sqn | CFB Uplands/CFB Bagotville/CFB Chatham | CG-101B/F |
| 425 Sqn | CFB Bagotville | CF-101B/F |

*Pacific Air Forces (PACAF)*

| | | |
|---|---|---|
| 15 TRS | Kadena AB, Okinawa | RF-101A/C |
| 20 TRS | Udorn RTAFB, Thailand [from TAC] | RF-101C |
| 45 TRS | Misawa AB, Japan/Tan Son Nhut AB, SVN | RF-101A/C |

*Tactical Air Command (TAC)*

| | | |
|---|---|---|
| 82 TATS | Tyndall AFB, Fla | F-101B/F |
| 481 FBS/ | | |
| 481 TFS | Bergstrom AFB, Tex | F-101A/C |
| 522 FBS/ | | |
| 522 TFS | Bergstrom AFB, Tex | F-101A/C |
| 523 FBS/ | | |
| 523 TFS | Bergstrom AFB, Tex | F-101A/C |
| 524 FBS/ | | |
| 524 TFS | Bergstrom AFB, Tex | F-101A/C |
| 17 TRS | Shaw AFB, SC [to USAFE] | RF-101A/C |
| 18 TRS | Shaw AFB, SC [to USAFE] | RF-101A/C |
| 20 TRS | Shaw AFB, SC [to PACAF] | RF-101C |
| 29 TRS | Shaw AFB, SC | RF-101A/C |
| 31 TRTS/ | | |
| 31 TRS | Shaw AFB, SC | RF-101A/C |
| 4414 CCTS | Shaw AFB, SC | RF-101A/C |
| 4416 TS | Shaw AFB, SC | RF-101A/C |

*United States Air Forces in Europe (USAFE)*

| | | |
|---|---|---|
| 17 TRS | Laon AB, France [from TAC] | RF-101A/C |
| 18 TRS | Laon AB, France/RAF Upper Heyford [from TAC] | RF-101A/C |
| 32 TRS | Phalsbourg AB, France | RF-101A/C |
| 38 TRS | Phalsbourg AB/France/Ramstein AB, Germany | RF-101A/C |
| 78 TFS | RAF Woodbridge, England | F-101A/C |
| 91 TFS | RAF Bentwaters, England | F-101A/C |
| 92 TFS | RAF Bentwaters, England | F-101A/C |

# Appendix 10: **RF-101C Voodoo Losses in Southeast Asia**

*Combat Losses:*

| | | | | |
|---|---|---|---|---|
| 21 Nov 64 | RF-101C | 56-0230 | 15 TRS | Lost in Laos |
| 03 Apr 65 | RF-101C | 56-0075 | 45 TRS Capt Hershel S (Scotty) Morgan | POW |
| 29 Apr 65 | RF-101C | 56-0190 | 15 TRS Capt Charles E Shelton | MIA |
| 06 May 65 | RF-101C | 56-0045 | 45 TRS Capt Robert A Stubberfield | Killed |
| 29 Jun 65 | RF-101C | 56-0401 | 15 TRS Capt Marvin N Lindsey | Killed |
| 29 Jul 65 | RF-101C | 56-0067 | 45 TRS Capt Jack W Weatherby | Killed |
| 13 Aug 65 | RF-101C | 56-0186 | 363 TRW Capt Frederic M Mellor | Killed |
| 27 Sep 65 | RF-101C | 56-0204 | 15 TRS Capt George R Hall | POW |
| 05 Oct 65 | RF-101C | 56-0175 | 15 TRS | Hit NVN; Rescued |
| 01 Nov 65 | RF-101C | 56-0174 | 15 TRS | NVN; Rescued |
| 26 Jan 66 | RF-101C | 56-0084 | 20 TRS | NVN; Rescued |
| 07 Mar 66 | RF-101C | 56-0043 | 45 TRS Capt Gordon L Page | Killed |
| 07 Mar 66 | RF-101C | 56-0220 | 15 TRS Capt Jerdy A Wright, Jr | Killed |
| 21 Mar 66 | RF-101C | 56-0066 | 45 TRS Capt Arthur W Burer | POW |
| 02 Apr 66 | RF-101C | 56-0172 | 45 TRS Major Daniel J Doughty | POW |
| 22 Apr 66 | RF-101C | 56-0090 | 20 TRS Major Alan L Brunston | POW |
| 29 Apr 66 | RF-101C | 56-0218 | 20 TRS Major Albert E Runyan | POW |
| 06 Jul 66 | RF-101C | 56-0051 | 20 TRS Major James F Young | POW |
| 31 Jul 66 | RF-101C | 56-0226 | 20 TRS Major William D (Dave) Burroughs | POW |
| 12 Aug 66 | RF-101C | 56-0056 | 20 TRS Major Blair G Wrye | Killed |
| 03 Nov 66 | RF-101C | 56-0175 | 45 TRS Lt Rogers | NVN; Rescued |
| 04 Nov 66 | RF-101C | 56-0093 | 30 TRS Capt Vincent J Connolly | Killed |
| 05 Dec 66 | RF-101C | 432 TRW | Capt Arthur L Warren | Killed |
| 08 Feb 67 | RF-101C | 56-0203 | 45 TRS | Hit NVN; Rescued |
| 20 May 67 | RF-101C | 56-0120 | 20 TRS Major Notley G Maddox | Killed |
| 07 Jul 67 | RF-101C | 56-0096 | 45 TRS | SVN; Rescued |
| 01 Aug 67 | RF-101C | 56-0207 | 20 TRS Capt Charles C Winston III | Killed |
| 16 Sep 67 | RF-101C | 56-0180 | 20 TRS Major Bobby R Bagley | POW |
| 16 Sep 67 | RF-101C | 56-0181 | 20 TRS | Hit NVN; cr Laos; Rescued |
| 18 Oct 67 | RF-101C | 56-0212 | 20 TRS | Laos; Rescued |
| 06 Aug 68 | RF-101C | 56-0215 | 45 TRS | Hit NVN; cr sea; Rescued |

*Operational Losses:*

| | | | | |
|---|---|---|---|---|
| 13 Apr 66 | RF-101C | 56-0086 | 20 TRS | Cr on landing |
| 26 Jul 66 | RF-101C | 56-0201 | (?) | Cr on landing |
| 07 Aug 66 | RF-101C | 56-0064 | 20 TRS | Flew into ground |
| 12 Mar 67 | RF-101C | 56-0063 | 20 TRS | Crashed |
| 09 Aug 67 | RF-101C | 56-0025 | 45 TRS | Collided with Army UH-1 |

*Ground Loss:*

| | | | | |
|---|---|---|---|---|
| 17 Feb 68 | RF-101C | 56-0182 | (45 TRS?) | Ground rocket attack |

# Specifications

## The First and the Last

**McDonnell XF-88 Voodoo** 46-525 c/n 1 11 August 1948

Type: single-seat penetration fighter

Powerplant: two 2,400-lb (1088-kg) thrust non-afterburning Westinghouse XJ34-W-13 turbojet engines

Performance: maximum speed 710 mph (1071 km/h) at 10,000 ft (3048 m); service ceiling 41,000 ft (12,496 m); range 1,000 miles (1609 km)

Weights: empty 26,100 lb (11,836 kg); maximum takeoff 39,995 lb (18,141 kg)

Dimensions: span 39 ft 8 in (12.09 m); length 54 ft 1 in (16.49 m); height 16 ft 3 in (4.93 m); wing area approx 340 sq ft (31.22 m$^2$)

Armament: none (four or six 20-mm cannons planned and installed on second airframe)

**McDonnell F-101B Voodoo** 59-478 c/n 802 circa. 1963

Type: two-seat all-weather interceptor

Powerplant: two 14,880-lb (6749-kg) thrust afterburning Pratt & Whitney J57-P-55 turbojet engines

Performance, maximum speed, 1,221 mph (1965 km/h) or Mach 1.85 at 40,000 ft (12,190 m); service ceiling 54,800 ft (16,705 m); range 1,550 miles (2494 km)

Weights: empty 28,970 lb (13,141 kg); maximum takeoff 52,400 lb (23,768 kg)

Dimensions: span 39 ft 8 in (12.09 m); length 67 ft 4¾ in (20.54 m); height 18 ft (5.49 m); wing area 368 sq ft (34.19 m$^2$)

Armament: two AIR-2A (MB-1) Genie rocket projectiles with nuclear warhead and four AIM-4C, -4D or -4G (GAR-8) Falcon infrared missiles, or six Falcon missiles

# Index